Social Work with Groups

LIBRARY OF SOCIAL WORK

GENERAL EDITOR: NOEL TIMMS
Lecturer in Social Science and Administration
London School of Economics

Social Work with Groups

by M. K. McCullough and P. J. Ely

LONDON
ROUTLEDGE & KEGAN PAUL
NEW YORK: HUMANITIES PRESS

First published 1968
by Routledge & Kegan Paul Ltd
Broadway House, 68-74 Carter Lane
London, E.C.4

Printed in Great Britain
by Northumberland Press Limited,
Gateshead

© *M. K. McCullough and P. J. Ely*

SBN 7100 6222 2 (C)
SBN 7100 6248 6 (P)

General editor's introduction

Owing to production delays this book was published in 1969

The Library of Social Work is designed to meet the needs of students following courses of training for social work. In recent years the number and kinds of training have increased in an unprecedented way. But there has been no corresponding increase in the supply of text-books to cover the growing differentiation of subject matter or to respond to the growing spirit of enthusiastic but critical enquiry into the range of subjects relevant to social work. The Library will consist of short texts designed to introduce the student to the main features of each topic of enquiry, to the significant theoretical contributions so far made to its understanding, and to some of the outstanding problems. Each volume will suggest ways in which the student might continue his work by further reading.

In the development of social work in this country emphasis has so far been given to social casework, even though some form of work with groups has been practised since the beginning of modern social work. As the authors of the present work suggest, social workers are now anxious to explore and develop skills in working with different kinds of groups. Such work has relevance in each of the specialist areas of social work, and for the increasing interest being shown in working with families. This book is divided into two parts: the first raises and discusses the practical problems that have to be faced when a social worker decides to work with a group, and describes some actual work undertaken in the field. The second part gives an account of the main theories that are considered to be helpful to the social worker. The authors see this division as a reflection of the situation in the field, where no one theory can be completely espoused and where the character of the social work situation heavily influences the application of any theory.

This book is devoted to the exploration of one of the methods of social work. Others in the series will consider aspects of social casework and of community work, which are usually seen as the two remaining methods adopted by social workers in the solution of the problems they meet. As these methods are expounded, it becomes clear that the usual terms (casework, groupwork, and community work) may prevent our seeing important similarities between social work methods, and that the interplay between the apparently simple notions of 'theory' and 'practice' is in fact complex.

NOEL TIMMS

Contents

Acknowledgement

The authors wish to acknowledge their debt for the help received in lectures, seminars and informal discussion from other social workers and from psychiatrists, and in particular from Dr. P. M. Turquet of the Tavistock Clinic who was also kind enough to read and advise on chapters two and three. They wish to make clear, however, that responsibility for the approach used is entirely theirs.

1

Description of Contents

This introduction to the practice of groupwork is intended
for social work students, although it is hoped that it will
also be of interest to experienced social caseworkers who
are considering making groupwork part of their professional practice. It is written in two parts: the first based
on practical experience in social work and the second on
the psychoanalytic theories which appear most relevant
to the understanding of group interaction. The work is
the product of collaboration between two authors, but
one (M. K. McCullough) has assumed major responsibility
for the first part of the book, and the other (P. J. Ely) for
the second. The division of the book accurately reflects the
present situation of groupwork in social work education
and practice.

No single theory either of groupwork practice or of
group dynamics is widely accepted, though an increasing
number of social workers are attempting to do at least
some of their work in groups. At the present stage of the
development of the subject it is peculiarly difficult to
describe the interplay of practice and theory. Social
workers look to the theories developed by other disciplines

for help either before or after they have tried to work with a group but, as the authors of this book indicate, the special conditions of social work must always be observed. It seemed best, therefore, to recognise some of the complexities of the working situation in the organisation of the book, and to avoid both distorting the practical experience so that it was made to look like the simple application of one or more theories, and over-simplifying the theoretical work to give a misleading list of apparently useful rules for groupwork.

There are many kinds of groups and things happen in all of them which involve the operation of group dynamics, just as all relationships between two people contain some of the factors involved in social casework. In this study, however, only that range of groupwork which is likely to be attempted by social workers will be described. In the first part of the book the approach is eclectic and descriptions of necessity simplified and generalised. The concepts and theories used are not original. The writers have gained valuable insight and stimulation from the writings of psychoanalysts and psychotherapists and from opportunities to discuss their work with them, but at the same time have kept realistically to the social work situation and reproduced and used only what they have found from experience to be applicable and helpful there. Technical terms and reference to specific group-analytic and other theoretical concepts have been carefully avoided in the first part of the book, so that the accounts should be comprehensible to the social work student with the help of his teachers, and make easy reading for a trained caseworker. It is hoped that the book will be of use to the beginning groupworker in understanding what is going on in groups as well as giving guidance in handling some of the situations which most commonly arise there.

This first chapter is concerned with some of the considerations, decisions and arrangements which must be made before a group is actually convened. The two following chapters look at some aspects of group dynamics from the point of view of practical experience; concentrating first on relationships between the group and the leader and then on relationships between members of the group. Groups in three different situations are described—with children, in an institution and as part of a training programme.

The latter part of the book is devoted to a review of the main psychoanalytical, and some alternative, approaches to groups and groupwork. Here, although every effort has been made to devise a straightforward and brief exposition, it has proved impossible to avoid the use of technical terms and concepts; these are, however, likely to be familiar to most social workers and to students after the first year of their studies. The student who wishes to extend his knowledge of groupwork is introduced to some of the more useful formulations of psychoanalytical writers. There is a summary of the ideas of Slavson, Foulkes, Bion, Ezriel and Stock Whitaker and Lieberman. There is also a brief indication of the relevance of these ideas to social work and a discussion of sociological factors in groups, with particular attention to the work of Homans, and a guide to further reading.

Settings for social groupwork

Groups may be held in a social worker's office and consist of the worker's own clients or of people he wishes to involve in understanding and helping them, perhaps members of the client's family, parents or marital partners.

Alternatively, groupwork may be done in residential institutions—for example, in a children's home, a hostel, a mental hospital, a school or a prison. Here the social worker taking the group may be a member of staff, as for example a psychiatric social worker in a mental hospital, or a visiting fieldworker, such as a child care officer in a children's home, or he may be someone who has no responsibility towards the institution or the residents other than that of conducting a group there.

Youth clubs and other leisure-time clubs are, of course, working with groups, but the term groupwork as used in this study would only be applicable to groups in youth clubs taken by social workers for the same general purposes as they would provide casework sessions. This would also be the case with 'unattached workers'—trained social workers who operate mainly in streets, cafes and pubs where natural groups congregate.

There are from time to time brief spontaneous groupings which a social worker with the requisite training and experience may be perceptive enough to recognise and use. In an institutional setting they may form naturally after some crisis, or just because the atmosphere is relatively relaxed and propitious, for example a group of boys travelling back to an institution after a match of some kind. These happenings in groupwork can be accepted and utilised valuably as can opportunities for short-term casework, but of course, as in casework, they are no substitute for systematic working together over a period.

Types of groupwork

Attempts have been made to define groupwork, to indicate the various ways in which it can be done and to differentiate clearly between them, but these are never entirely

4

satisfactory. It is a comparatively new subject, and people of various professions and nationalities working in many agencies in differing ways are engaged on it without much opportunity for general comparison and discussion. This incoherence is reflected in the varieties of terms used to describe kinds of social groupwork of which the most common are group therapy, group guidance and group counselling. The relevant literature often attempts to define these but in talking and writing about their work practitioners tend to choose whichever term they find most attractive, so that a social worker may use the term 'group therapy' to describe work he is doing which he feels to be in some depth, while another will use 'group counselling' to describe much the same kind of work. The term used, therefore, is not always a precise indication of the kind of work done.

To avoid involvement in controversy and to prevent further misunderstanding the writers will use the term 'social groupwork' throughout. It is not intended to apply to any precisely defined technique, but to cover the range of activities of a social worker in a group in the same way that 'social casework' covers his activities in the one-to-one situation.

Social workers will find in the literature a number of differing, even conflicting, theories and a wide variety of practice. However, there are a number of things which are more or less generally agreed, particularly in considering the more practical aspects of the situation, and the remainder of this introductory chapter will be devoted to them.

Number of members in the group

There must be enough people for group interaction to take

place but not so many that the leader and the members cannot be aware of each other simultaneously. Two people, or three, limit interaction to simple association and rivalry, so four might be a minimum. On the other hand, a dozen people together all talking and reacting produces rather a confused picture, so perhaps there should not be more than nine or ten people in a group. In practice the number seven seems to be about right, and perhaps its traditional, magical religious significance may not be unrelated to the fact that it is a good number for any kind of group. It has come to be the accepted norm in the kind of group-work with which we are mainly concerned. One or two less perhaps in a play group for disturbed children, two or three more if desired in an adolescent or adult discussion group.

Regularity and frequency of meetings

Meetings must be held at regular intervals, and even an occasional cancellation has repercussions in the group. An unreliable group programme will be interpreted by the members as a demonstration of indifference and lack of interest on the part of the leader, and they will react by withdrawal, hostility or depression. The frequency of meetings will depend partially on the organisation of the agency and the time available. Meetings at four-week intervals might in some circumstances be useful, though the group would tend to lose impetus in the long gaps. There is a great deal to be said for regular weekly meetings. More frequent sessions would be impracticable in most settings but may sometimes be possible—for example for social workers employed in institutions.

Length of each session

Sessions are usually fixed at between one and two hours. In group work a considerable swing and variation in interest and pace is usual, so that on some occasions an hour will pass all too quickly and on others it will seem very long indeed. Group leaders may decide to finish the group early or to extend it at their discretion, or alternatively keep strictly to the pre-arranged time. The advantages of flexibility are obvious and tempting: one is spared boredom in a dull session and can prolong one which is going well, but there are advantages in keeping to the set time. It gives security and has the practical advantage that both the leader and the group are free to make plans for the period after the group. It must be remembered that something is *always* happening in a group; boredom and long silences probably mean resistance and difficulties which the group will need to work through before they can go on. Closing the group early just avoids the issue.

Number of group meetings

The practice of groupwork, like that of casework, allows for short as well as long-term work. Nevertheless, time is needed for group interaction to manifest itself and be worked through usefully. Although help can sometimes be given in one or two sessions, where circumstances permit a group project should be planned to last over a longish period, for example weekly meetings for at least three months or if possible for a year or more. As in casework there is no steady onward movement from trivial to significant, rather advance and retreat, progression and regression. Sometimes important things happen quite early

SWG—B   7

in the life of a group but there is no way of inducing this. If a reasonable time is allowed the group has a chance to proceed at its own pace.

Closed and open groups

Before starting a group it is as well to decide whether it is to be a 'closed' or 'open' group. A closed group starts and finishes with the same people, and if anyone drops out he is not replaced. An open group adds members, and loses them, for various reasons as it goes along. A closed group is in some ways easier to run because changes are disruptive and disturbing to the group. On the other hand, the phenomena they provide can be good material for the group to work on. In any case the realities of some social workers' settings with cases being handled for only a short time may make an open group the only practicable one.

Room and equipment

Groups must be held in a room where there will be no interruptions either in person or by telephone, and where a good deal of noise can be made without disturbing others. A chair each, and possibly a small table, are all that is needed for a discussion group. In the case of a play group for children, all valuable and breakable objects must be removed, the fire guarded and material for imaginative play provided—details of this will be found in a later chapter.

Selection

Selection for groupwork is much discussed in the literature and there are many views. Among these are:

(a) Groups should consist of people who have patterns of personality and problems in common.

8

(b) No two members of a group should be alike, thus giving the greatest possible spread and variety of person and problem.

(c) Members should be paired for similarity of personality or problem so that each should be able to identify with one other person while the group still provides variety.

(d) Members should all have the same presenting symptom.

More general considerations of age, sex, intelligence, education and degree of disturbance will always have to be considered.

The realities of most social workers' situations however, do not give much opportunity for selection. Some people are obviously unsuitable. For example, a social worker's group would not include the seriously mentally ill unless psychiatric supervision is available. In practice it is often possible to bring together people who have a roughly similar presenting problem and to ignore more subtle diagnostic considerations. Then, in effect, one has a mixed group.

Social workers are free to choose casework, or groupwork, or a combination of the two as the best method of helping a client, and it is probably better at this stage not to be too specific about the criteria to be used, leaving each worker to make decisions based on their understanding of their clients' problems, as long as they are prepared to reconsider their decision at a later stage if circumstances appear to warrant it.

Preparation

Most social workers will start by familiarising themselves

with a sketch of each member's history and problems before starting the group, although there is a school of thought which favours starting 'blind'. Group members, too, should understand the purpose and scope of the group before they commit themselves to it. This may be difficult, particularly when speaking to children or unsophisticated adults, but it is important to be honest. Children may be asked to come to a play group 'so that we can all get to know one another better and help each other'; *not* just that they will learn to paint, or love playing with the toys, or learn a new hobby. Adults can be given an explanation adjusted to their particular circumstances which also makes clear that in the group it is hoped that they will be able to obtain help with their difficulties while at the same time helping others.

Recording

There are difficulties in making detailed and accurate reports of groupwork, as there are in casework. Some workers take notes during the group, but as far as the writers are concerned this has seemed even more inhibiting and distracting to the clients than it does in casework. The realities of most social workers' situations make elaborate plans for typing verbatim from tapes impractical except perhaps for short experimental periods. A brief résumé written as soon after the group as possible would seem the most practical solution, but groupworkers will have to find their own preferred method. Whatever the method, recording is important. Groupwork, because of the multiplicity of factors involved, is particularly difficult to assess clearly, and confusing to think about. Systematic recording, however brief, helps the worker to recognise recurring themes, to see patterns in behaviour and so on. It is also invaluable if there is going to be any opportunity for discussion with other groupworkers, and for supervision.

Closing a group

This can be difficult, and is always deserving of careful handling. The group tends to intensify feeling and the closing of the group means not only a parting between worker and client, as it does in casework, but each member loses the support of the rest of the group. It can be taken as a little death and treated with due ceremony. On the other hand, some groups, like old soldiers, 'never die but only fade away'; they dwindle or come to a natural end as members move away or their circumstances change.

In whatever way the end of a group is reached, members do seem to feel some sense of loss. The closing of a group should therefore be discussed well in advance so that feeling can be expressed—for example, by staying away. In some circumstances it may be thought desirable for the worker to keep individual contact with members after the group has ended. Members themselves sometimes try to keep up an association after the official group has finished, but this would seem to have a certain unreality, and does not often last for long. The desire to prolong the treatment situation is presumably a sign that the member is not ready, or willing, to finish treatment, and plenty of opportunity to discuss and live through the situation must therefore be given beforehand, including an opportunity to show any feeling of resentment and anger which may be felt towards the groupworker as the person responsible for the ending of the group.

2

Group interaction—the leader's role

The pattern of interaction in a group is complex and multi-dimensional and therefore difficult to analyse, and the description which follows is of necessity simplified and incomplete. Each member brings to the group his inherited characteristics and his life experience, and these will colour his perceptions of and reactions to the other group members and the leader. He will project into the group patterns of relationships established at earlier stages of his life, and this means that, besides the real group, there are as many different fantasy-groups as there are members.

For the sake of clarity this chapter will deal mainly with the leader's role in the group and the members' relationships with him, and the next with their relationships with each other. In reality these two sections are so closely woven together in the fabric of the group that it is almost impossible to separate them out.

Beginning a group

The question of selection has been discussed in chapter one. At the first meeting of a new group, the worker will give some information about himself to the group. They

may know him already or have met him in the course
of the selection procedure, and how much he should tell
them will vary in different circumstances. However, the
group has a right to know why he is there, and to have
a chance to ask him questions about himself and his function. The guiding lines as to how fully these should be
answered are those which are followed by social workers
in all professional relationships.

Members should be introduced to each other by whatever method the leader's commonsense deems appropriate.
With children it may be enough just to mention first
names; they will probably ask for information to enable
them to 'place' each other—what school they attend, what
street they live in. Adolescents and adults may like to introduce themselves giving their names and adding, if they
wish, a little information about their job or school, their
family and so on. Quite apart from the practical utility
of this procedure, it makes a familiar, ritual beginning for
group interaction.

The leader should then repeat the explanation of the task
of the group which has been given to members individually. This should be clear enough for members to understand and to enable them to consent again, as a group, to
the purpose of the group, but not so precise that they will
feel that they have been given an agenda which they must
follow. The explanation can be very generalised; to understand ourselves or to discuss a particular kind of problem.
Once a group has got under way the problems peculiar
to any particular group will be pin-pointed by the members themselves.

For example, the leader could say 'as was explained in
the individual interviews, you have been asked if you
would like to come together to talk about the difficulties

you have, and to try and help one another'. This tells people what the group is about—i.e. that it is not a social or teaching session—but at the same time room is left for a spread of discussion. Or, in a group selected because they have a specific problem in common 'you have been asked to come together because it was felt that you would be able to understand and help one another, and that I might be able to help you with the questions which arise in . . .' (e.g. rearing a mongol child).

The worker will give the group his relaxed courteous attention, saying as little as possible, especially at first, and that designed to facilitate the communications of others. At first most groups members tend to direct their remarks to the leader, thus bringing to the group not only a repetition of family relationships, but patterns of behaviour learned in earlier life, for example in the classroom. The groupworker can help to break this pattern by encouraging members to comment on each other's statements. The group is unstructured and the groupworker non-directive and permissive. This means that members are not given roles to play, the worker does not direct the group's activities, and he permits the group to behave in ways which might be inappropriate in other settings.

Silence, tension and resistance are natural phenomena in any group. Most groups start cold, shy and silent and are often quietly hostile. They do not know the leader and each other, and they are not sure how to behave. Many groups stay like this over a long period, or become so again after very revealing emotionally loaded sessions when members perhaps feel that they have gone too far. They may seem determined to chatter about trivialities, which is another kind of silence. This experience, like everything else which happens in a group, must be accepted and

14

worked through. Silence can be very trying to the group and to the leader, but it can also be very positive, a breathing space in which feelings develop, reservations are overcome, and people come to terms with what is happening in the group. Pauses will usually be broken by one of the group members; if this does not happen the leader will use his own judgement as to how and when to intervene. This decision like many others, will have to be made bearing in mind among other things the type of member selected and the leader's training and experience. There is no hard and fast rule, and a social worker will not necessarily imitate the long enigmatic silences of some group analysts. When, where and how much the leader will need to intervene to stimulate discussion and to help group members to put their feelings into words will vary a great deal. A good rough rule would be to comment on what is happening in the group rather than to introduce a new subject.

This last is of basic importance because, in a group, what is happening should be *allowed* to happen, so that the group will arrive from time to time at areas of real concern to some or all of its members. A group leader is not a chairman keeping the group to his agenda, however admirable a document this might be. He helps communication rather as one helps water to flow downhill, that is by removing obstacles from its path. So if a group dries up or gets sticky he may direct the members' attention to what is happening, saying for example, 'we are quiet to-night' or 'this subject seems to give rise to a good deal of anxiety' rather than 'well, lets talk about something else'.

Comment and interpretation

The groupworker can sometimes perceive what lies behind

a member's words or actions and have insight into his anxieties and difficulties. To give a simple example, behind a member's bitter complaint of the rudeness of a shop assistant, told with inappropriate distress or anger, may lie resentment against something, real or fantasied, done by the groupworker which is felt to be too dangerous to express directly. Behind this again may be glimpsed a pattern of feeling and reaction probably originally established in early childhood relationships with the member's father or mother.

The groupworker's perception may be quite mistaken, but from time to time he will make what he can feel to be reasonably shrewd and informed guesses as to what is really happening in the group, based on his knowledge of human behaviour and motivation in general, of the group members in particular, and of the processes of group interaction. Even if matters go no further than this, the process has some value, because the worker's understanding of, and sympathy towards, the member is increased, and in an ongoing relationship this can be helpful in a variety of ways.

To continue with the example above the groupworker could, if he considered it appropriate suggest to the member that perhaps he was also angry with the worker because of such and such a thing, always remembering that these interventions only have value if they are at the same time relevant, understandable and acceptable to the client. The groupworker cannot *give* his insight into a problem to the person concerned. In the emotionally loaded field of personal relationships it is not just a question of what is true, it is a matter of what can be absorbed and accepted.

In a group, interventions are not usually directed exclusively to one particular member. To do so may be so

16

anxiety-provoking that the member is quite unable to take in what is being said. The comment can be framed so that it is addressed to the group and yet understood by the member for whom it is intended. This sometimes has the added advantage that another member with similar problems of which the group leader is not at the time aware, can also be helped. Interventions should be very simple and brief and not contain more than one idea at a time. If they are too long and too complicated, members will not understand and absorb them.

The groupworker can feed into the group those points which he feels will help the group to keep to its task and to clarify what it is doing. Another way in which he does this is by helping the group to pause from time to time and consider what has been happening and where they have arrived. These summaries contribute to the group memory.

The worker must bring to the group his full and concentrated attention, his training and experience, his knowledge of humanity in general and his clients in particular, and his goodwill. This goodwill consists not only of a desire to help, but of a willingness to be attacked, and to talk about and also to initiate discussion of difficult and painful things. He must be willing to be tested out and to allow the group to come to terms with him in its own way. He must, especially at first, be prepared to sit back and let the group come to life. The members will take over the situation and live in it so that both their immediate preoccupations and difficulties and some of the predisposing reasons for these can be brought to the surface. While this is happening the worker must be receptive, and his comments will be directed towards helping things along rather than controlling them. He must accept that it is how the members react to the group that matters and that at best he

17

can only help them to help themselves. The very fact that a person is able to make a significant communication which is accepted by the leader and the group is in itself therapeutic because it involves both the relief of tension and some degree of self-understanding. Members should be allowed to develop and repeat their themes at their own pace. The leader can only usefully deal with what they bring to the group and must not try to drag out in too determined a manner matters they do not feel able to discuss at that time.

Interpretation and clarification are terms used freely and in a variety of different ways in social work. They are applied, for example, to the translation by the worker into plain words of unconscious material, acted out or verbalised symbolically by the client, and at the other extreme helping the inarticulate client to put into words a feeling or an opinion of which he is perfectly conscious and which he is willing but unable to communicate clearly. Between these two extremes is a range of activity which is part of the practice of trained and experienced caseworkers, among the most common being the interpretation of conscious material which the client feels is too dangerous to express directly. It is also quite common to find that punitive, didactic or moralistic attitudes frowned on in casework teaching reappear under the label of interpretation. For example, a social worker may say to a boy who constantly irritates and provokes others 'no wonder that you are always complaining that other boys hit you at school, if you annoy them like that all the time'. This is a criticism of the child and as such may be accurate enough. If he has formed a positive relationship with the worker it may help him to modify his behaviour. It is not, however, an interpretation because it does not clarify
18

or take further what the child is expressing. A much simpler remark could be an interpretation. 'You are trying to make the other boy angry' or 'you are trying to make him hit you', or 'you want to be sure of his attention even if it means being hurt'. Taking it a little further it might at some stage be appropriate to relate such behaviour to the boy's feelings with regard to the worker and at another time to his relationship with his family.

Interpretation can be offered to link fantasy with reality. A ten year old West Indian boy, whose relationship with the groupworker was highly ambivalent, constantly drew witches and talked about them in such a way that it was clear that he identified her as a witch. Eventually she said, 'you mean that you think I am a witch, then?' He remained silent and avoided her eye but settled down to draw another witch picture, this time with a small figure beneath. The worker asked it he thought that the witch was going to swoop on that person and he said no, she was a good witch, kind to children and animals. When asked where the witch was going on her broomstick, he said that she was going to tea with another witch—an admission that the worker's aims were probably benevolent and her life outside the group (about which he questioned her a great deal at one stage) blameless and respectable enough. After this his relationship with the groupworker grew affectionate and positive, although he never quite abandoned his witch symbol.

Group members may offer explanations of their behaviour in symbolic form. Another West Indian, a boy of twelve, had been separated from his father for a long period and was then sent by his mother from the West Indies to join his father and stepmother. At twelve he was a withdrawn, rather dignified boy who seldom spoke. In the group he warmed and relaxed only very gradually and any expression of feeling came as a result of a visible struggle. At one session he put his own position beautifully to the group. 'There is a dog in our street who chases cats. He has forgotten, you see?' The groupworker did not see, and asked various and, as it turned out, quite irrelevant questions. The boy struggled on and after several false starts, said: 'Once a cat chased the dog and bloodied its nose. He couldn't remember which cat so every time he saw a cat he thought: "That's the cat that bloodied my nose" and he chased it'. It was felt that too direct an interpretation might have been unacceptable to this child, but a generalisation to the whole group about people whose feelings had been hurt being reluctant to risk making friends was accepted and mutual understanding at last reached.

Interpretation can also be used to link symbolic play in the group with real life outside. Fantastic accounts by delinquent boys, told or acted out, about robbing banks and so on can be related, if group relationships are good, to actual misdemeanours outside the group. Here group members will reinforce reality, discussing one another's behaviour, truthfulness and sincerity with cheerful thoroughness.

In the group fantasies the worker is often the stand-in for real people in the members' lives outside, commonly a parent, and will from time to time be treated in a way which may be quite inappropriate to his actual behaviour but appropriate to that of the person he represents. If necessary this can be recognised and put into words, 'You are angry with me, because you think that I . . . (treat you as a baby, am trying to force you to do something you don't want to do, don't like you etc.) or it may be considered desirable to take matters a step further. 'Are you angry because you think I am behaving as your father used to?' As with all interpretations, therapeutic value depends not only on accuracy but on appropriateness at any particular stage, and the same interpretation, so helpful if offered at the right moment, may be irrelevant or superfluous earlier or later.

So, for the social worker, the amount and kind of interpretation he makes in a group depends on what, in the situation, he judges to be helpful. It must be remembered too that the group members will share in this, as in other, therapeutic functions.

Non-verbal communication

Communication in a group will not always flow easily. There may be periods of change and activity when the leader and the group members will feel that a lot of ground has been covered and some understanding achieved. In any but the most superficial of group projects, there will also be periods of boredom, frustration and resistance, and of false or camouflage activity ranging from social chat to trying to be whatever sort of group they imagine the leader would like them to be. The leader will listen and clarify or interpret if opportunity arises. Sometimes there will be very little said for him to interpret, and the leader must develop his sensitivity to non-verbal communication.

A great deal happens in groups, and indeed in the world at large, which is not put into words. It is a common experience of ordinary life that the most important things people need to say to each other are difficult, if not impossible, to put into words and the more emotionally loaded the communication the more indirectly it is sometimes made. We all know that feelings and reactions to others are conveyed by facial expression, by tone of voice, (as distinct from what is said), gestures, bodily movement, and often, most significantly, by silence and stillness.

When this kind of non-verbal communication occurs in a group the leader will note it and may consider it appropriate to comment. It may be the only communication an inarticulate person is going to make, so that the leader may say to the member who throws himself back in his chair, turning his face away from the group. 'You don't agree with what is being said, John?' and give him a chance to put his feelings into words if he wishes without dragging him too clumsily into the discussion.

The groupworker as leader

The worker functions, and is perceived by the members, as a person having authority. The fact that he chooses not to exercise it in the usual way does not mean that it is not there. A permissive technique implies that authority is implicit in the situation. One cannot permit unless one has the potential to prevent, and permissiveness is by no means to be equated with helplessness.

Social workers used to talk as if authority operated only in certain agencies, for example those dealing with delinquents. In fact, all agencies have some sort of authority with regard to their clients. Even a voluntary agency has the authority to accept an applicant or refuse him service, to give or with-hold the help he asks for. Child care officers, psychiatric social workers, welfare officers and so on, all have authority. They have the authority of their agency, of their special knowledge, and above all they have the authority with which their clients projective fantasies invest them.

22

The earliest and most impressive representatives of authority whom we meet are our parents or their substitutes, and this experience, with our inherited qualities will condition our attitude towards those who at least for a time, fulfil important roles in our lives. In the group, as in life generally, there is a tendency to superimpose this pattern of reaction onto the objective realities of the present environment. Patterns carried over from early social experience at school, at work and elsewhere will also recur in the group.

The more insight a group member can obtain, and the more he is aware of what he is doing, the greater his chance of bringing his reactions into line with reality and modifying and controlling his behaviour.

A group member's stand in relation to the leader as a parent or authority figure, whether dependant or hostile, will often emerge clearly quite soon after a group has started, and in some cases the leader will be conscious of quite definite reciprocal feelings of like and dislike towards particular members. Social workers are only human, and the desire to pay back an attacking member is natural enough. The important thing is that it should be consciously recognised for what it is.

The leader is, by reason of his function, isolated in the group, and in most group projects there are periods when this becomes very obvious. Resulting feelings of depression and hopelessness are experienced by most groupworkers from time to time and these, too, must be accepted as part of the group experience.

What *kind* of leader is the social groupworker? This is a difficult question and an answer making a narrow definition is neither possible nor desirable, because workers will operate in different ways and groups have different needs.

Efforts to give some sort of description are reflected in the terms in common use in groupwork literature, like convenor and conductor.

What kinds of leaders are there? There is the traditional gallant young officer galloping at the head of his troop, leading by the example of his bravery, by his superior knowledge—he knew which way they were supposed to go—and by authority because he could order them forward and shoot anyone who disobeyed. This authority was already well established and constituted and the external pressure of the enemy on his group would tend to support it, at least as long as things were going well. Group leadership in the sort of groups we are discussing does not resemble this.

Then there is the conductor of an orchestra. He knows the score and keeps the group to it. He is aware of every member and has their full attention so that they may function well together. This kind of leadership has points of similarity with the group leader, but it is in many ways very different because the groupworker does *not* know the score except in the very broadest sense. His skill lies in the difficult dual task of helping members to function as part of the group and benefit from it while at the same time leaving them free to arrive at the consideration of their problems and their possible solution in their own way and at their own pace.

Another kind of leader is the mob leader, the rabble rouser, the leader who knows what he wants the men to do and has enough understanding of human beings and skill in handling them to get at least some of them to follow him. He may achieve some group objective but he does not benefit the group members as individuals except very indirectly.

A fourth alternative is a more passive sort of leader altogether—the bus conductor. He is responsible for the bus,

24

he brings it along and controls it. He says who shall be allowed to get on, directs when and where the bus will stop and start, and takes the fares. He does not control where you sit or who you talk to or what you say or do unless it seriously inconveniences others. In many ways this sort of leader is nearest of the four to a social group-worker. He must, however, do more than provide the group, decide who shall join it and where it shall be held and then keep it running, like a bus conductor. He must try to help each member to gain insight, to relieve tension and anxiety, and grow towards maturity. To do this he must function in the group as one who releases and encourages real communication. He must also take responsibility for group policy, and for the boundaries which he sets for it. For example, he will work to avoid major hurts to his group members, but accept responsibility for the minor hurts which are inseparable from change and growth.

Some groups are run with more than one leader. There may be two leaders of equal status, and for this to be suc-cessful there must be good mutual understanding and some previous agreement on technique and aims; the relationship should be sufficiently secure for an occasional disagree-ment to be discussed in the group. There are settings in which joint leadership may be desirable, and it has at least two advantages. It offers the group a choice of roles for the leaders—most usually mother and father to the group—and it gives the leaders a mutual experience on which to com-pare notes, to pool insight and to discuss possible interpre-tations.

It is sometimes arranged that a leader will sit with some-one whose status and role in the group is secondary, usually with someone who is there to gain experience of group-work. Here again mutual understanding and agreement is essential, so that the impact of the second person in the group is utilised. A group tends to resent the secondary leader, at least at first, and see him as a strong rival for the leader's attention and affection, whether he is perceived as the leader's partner (husband-wife) or his favourite child.

It is impossible to ignore the presence of the second leader in the group. In some clinics one way screens and microphones are installed for teaching purposes so that students may observe without disturbing the group members, although with their knowledge. In a social work agency the best way of introducing another worker or a student into the group either as a participant or non-participant member is to give the group a simple and true explanation of why he is there and thereafter to accept him as part of the group experience.

The leader can never be conscious of everything that happens in the group. At any one time he may only be aware of a tiny fraction of it or he may completely misunderstand what he sees and hears. It may even appear that nothing is happening at all, but it could also mean that what is happening is hidden. Just what is being concealed, why, and by whom, is a matter for speculation, and possibly the concealment itself may be commented upon. At other times so much is happening that the leader scarcely has time to glimpse it in passing. He may be like the lookout man on a becalmed ship who watches the horizon for days without seeing any movement at all, and at other times, like the pilot of a boat shooting the narrow channels of a dangerous stretch of rapids, watching for rocks and whirlpools and the deceptively smooth slick of shallow water over stone. Then of necessity he can only watch the area through which the group is currently plunging with no attention to spare for the past or the surrounding terrain. Understanding of what is happening in the group and inspiration as to helpful interpretation may not come until long after the meeting is finished, and so not be immediately helpful yet it is valuable in the long-term life of the group because it will illumine subsequent events.

One comfort is that if the leader does allow a communication which is important to the group to pass unnoticed, the chances are that they will return to the subject later because it is too vital to be left unanswered. At times this will become very obvious as a group reverts again and again to a problem or grievance, like a needle stuck in the groove of a gramophone record, until the leader, or someone else in the group, grasps what is happening, and is able to discuss it.

The group leader must want to help his members, not just observe or diagnose them. He must try to have this positive feeling towards each and every group member, although some will be more naturally attractive and congenial to him than others. He will need to be prepared for a long journey into uncharted country, meeting much difficulty and a good deal of hostility and aggression as well as affection and some success. He must be the sort of traveller who is not unduly worried because, although he knows roughly which way he is going, he is not sure of the precise path, and can accept that at times he will be bogged down and at others travelling round in circles. He will not, in one sense, be leading the group at all. He is a fellow-traveller, more knowledgeable and less personally involved than the others, a person to be referred to and depended upon, but also to be blamed and attacked if the group seems to have lost its way.

The group will provide its own experience for the members. The leader's function is to help them to benefit from it.

3

Group interaction—the group members

Once again, it must be remembered that interaction between the group members is inextricably mixed with interaction between the leader and the group, and that in any situation these two aspects cannot be separated or even clearly distinguished. The distinction has been made to simplify matters for the reader, not to perpetuate an artificial distinction.

Group roles

One way of looking at the group situation is to think of the group as a stage, and the members as actors, each of whom can choose his own role according to his character and problems and the use he is going to make of the group. In the sort of unstructured, permissive group we have been describing there is no script and no stage director. Some will take leading parts, some quite literally supporting roles and one or two may act or mime their determination *not* to be involved. Over a period of time, some members will act the same part but others will change. Members may compete for a role or take turns in it. In a group of delinquent boys, for example, one may take the role of the favourite child and keep it throughout while another boy may work through aggression and violence to a more positive and affectionate relationship with the leader and the group. A boy who has previously behaved in a rather timid and even effeminate way may then take the role he has vacated, becoming much more aggressive and masculine.

Seating positions

One way in which members reflect their choice of role in the group is in their seating position in relation to the groupworker. It is a good idea for the latter to sit in the same place at each meeting, although formal 'head of the table' seating should be avoided. This means that should members arrive before the worker does they know where he is likely to sit and can choose their place accordingly. After one or two meetings, seating positions settle down to a fairly clear pattern, and then a change in place is likely to accompany a change in the member's feeling and behaviour. Provided that the room is arranged in the same way before each meeting starts the members can rearrange it in a way that reflects what is happening in the group, for example moving towards or away from the leader, or removing an absent member's chair from the circle and sitting closer together, perhaps feeling attacked by his defection.

People who depend on the groupworker for support and protection tend to sit near him, and it sometimes seems that active supporters sit on his right and passive on the left, but this may be accidental. A member who is finding the group a threatening experience may sit well back in a corner.

In the boys' play group described in chapter four members seldom sat down all at once, but the boys who for the time being were displaying the most active and uncontrolled behaviour often played at the far end of the the small room, sometimes with the male groupworker. The boy currently playing the part of the baby of the family or the favourite child would get as near to the female worker as he could, sometimes even lying on the floor under the table at her feet. The member who fulfils the role of favourite child may behave in an elaborately good way or may mildly provocative to gain attention.

Choice of seating position, then, is a form of non-verbal communication, and the groupworker can interpret if he feels it would be helpful to do so. It must be borne in mind, however, that it is non-verbal indirect communication just because it is something the group does not feel able at that time to communicate directly, and so it may be best to take it up indirectly, by a generalised comment offered to the group as a whole.

The self-appointed leader

People who are going to offer themselves as opposition leaders generally sit opposite the groupworker, often with a supporter or second-in-command beside them. They may attack the leader quite openly, criticising him and the way he conducts the group, or they may do so by elaborate demonstrations of boredom, inappropriate amusement or laboured politeness. Another kind of self-appointed leader takes on a supporting role towards the groupworker, misunderstanding or fearing the consequences of his permissiveness and attempting to control the group or explain the leader's wishes to them. Yet others appoint themselves

30

as group spokesmen and try to act as the only channel of communication from the group to the leader.

Reflection shows that these are standardised ways of behaving towards an authority figure who represents, as we have seen, a long line starting with parents and ending with those in our present environment, police, employers and so on. There is the person who is so afraid that he must attack at sight without waiting to see if he is in actual danger. There is the one whose experiences have left him with deep distrust and to whom the only defence against further betrayal is an elaborate show of non-involvement. There is the person who can only cope with life if it is stabilised into a pattern of relationships with which he is familiar; he is threatened by the leader's permissiveness. And there are people who in any particular group cannot quite take leading positions but who are seconds in command enjoying their chosen leader's protection and, vicariously, his prowess. It sometimes happens that a leader changes his role and then his lieutenant, stranded, is left to flounder until he finds another place for himself in the group.

Group members will deal with these situations in a wide variety of ways, and whether or not a self-appointed leader is accepted as such depends partly on whether he really represents the feeling of a substantial number of the members. Changes of feeling in the group may be marked by the fall of one self-appointed leader and the rise of another of a different type.

The scapegoat

Most groups at some time in their existence produce a scapegoat. This word refers to the primitive practice in which the collective sins of the community were loaded onto a person or animal who was then driven out into the wilderness. A group may project its collective badness onto one member; he talks too much, he is stupid, destructive, rude and hostile towards the leader, or he is unduly servile and ingratiating. In short he offends against the group mores, doing all the bad things other members would at times like to do themselves. The rejection of the scapegoat varies in intensity and venom. In extreme cases the member so treated may actually feel obliged to leave the group. The social groupworker must take responsibility for this as for everything else that happens in the group. The situation can be allowed time to develop until the group members them-selves can begin to see what is happening. Interpretation along the lines indicated in the previous chapter may then be helpful. Direct intervention to protect the scapegoat will not usually be necessary, but here of course the leader must use his discretion as the experience might be damag-ing to a particularly vulnerable member. Very often how-ever the group chooses with a certain shrewdness. The scapegoat may offer himself for the role as surely as does the self-appointed leader, and display the sort of behaviour only too likely to call down hostility and rejection from his fellows. The group experience can then be positive and helpful for him in that the pattern of hostile behaviour and consequent rejection is not simply repeated, but this time it can be examined and discussed in the group. The scapegoat may come to see what has happened and the rest recognise their projections. Even without much in the way of interpretation there seems to be a tendency for this to happen. Groups relent towards their scapegoat and re-instate him in their esteem, sometimes going off in full cry after another.

Sub-groups

Sub-groups develop in most groups and will often arrange to meet outside the group, have a coffee or walk to the bus together. Efforts are sometimes made to prevent this, but it is very a natural thing to happen. The groupworker must accept it as a part of the group experience and as occasion arises draw the group's attention to what is happening. Members are feeding information to each other and not to the whole group, and if the leader and the group do not know what is going on they cannot help. In extreme circumstances sub-grouping can be destructive and vitiate the whole life of the group.

The recurring theme

Individuals, or sometimes the whole group, have chronic anxieties and recurring problems which their discussion will reach from the most unlikely starting points and return to after ranging widely. Other things which happen will be adapted to fit this preoccupation, and the subject will recur in various disguises. It can be rather like listening to a piece of music in which a theme is developed. It may be repeated in turn by different instruments and appear in different forms, faster or slower, louder or quieter, embroidered or inverted. Sometimes the whole orchestra sweeps forward with the theme, at others it will be heard on one instrument only. A different idea may engage the attention of the orchestra for a time, but the original one will reappear in the bass line as a sort of subterranean mutter. These recurring themes are of importance both diagnostically, as they may give a clue to the inner meaning of behaviour, and therapeutically, because of the catharsis

33

and insight which may be achieved. At the very least the group can recognise a shared problem and know that it can be discussed and that they do not suffer alone.

The group as a whole

The group appears at times to have a life and personality of its own. Three kinds of relationship exist in the group, those between group members as individuals, between individual members and the groupworker, and between the group as a whole and individual members or the leader. Relationships of individuals with the group as a whole tend to develop a little later than the others.

The group will at times unite to support or condemn a member and will sometimes show a united front towards the leader. It may mother a member, nurse him as it were, reassure him and put him right, or at other times reject him, as in the scapegoat situation. Members may use the group for purposes of projection, as if it had a corporate life of its own. There is, of course, nothing new in this idea. We speak of the family as having a life of its own, and such terms as team spirit are in common use.

The group may grasp the significance of what a member has to say faster and more accurately than the worker, and distinguish better, for example, mock aggression from real anger, real depression from attention-seeking mournful behaviour. They can also recognise truth with remarkable shrewdness. They may be a peer-group and it is quite possible that they may know one another outside the group, living in the same neighbourhood, or attending the same schools. In institutional groups they will eat and sleep together.

Another aspect of the group as a whole is that it often

34

seems more intelligent and perceptive and to have a more positive and normal attitude to life than is possessed by the individual members. A group of delinquent boys, anti-authority and with low average intelligence, will in an unstructured group swiftly construct a set of norms for themselves and observe them carefully. Violent expression of aggression may be part of the group play, but no one is actually hurt.

The group will comment on the behaviour of a member who is testing out the situation. He is too rough, or he *needs* to break things, he is spoiling their game, he is stealing the play material, he is behaving like a two year old and so on. They rarely, however, reject him. They wait to walk home together, ask after him if he stays away and welcome him back. In fact their tolerance and affection may sometimes put the worker to shame.

It is possible to suggest a number of reasons for the fact that the group appears to be more intelligent, mature and stable than the people who constitute it. Members have different strengths and weaknesses, and perhaps they supply one another's deficiencies. They may also identify with the worker and incorporate some of his qualities and attitudes. Meantime the group is offering its own norms and its corrective social experience. This is at times in conflict with the members' lives outside, and this conflict may be recognised in the group. One group of delinquent girls in an institution, arguing fiercely among themselves about bullying, maintained that some fighting was inevitable. When the worker commented that such behaviour might be considered more appropriate to boys than young women they hastened to assure her, with some amusement, that they would never dream of fighting in front of her, and went on to discuss with some insight their mixed feelings about adolescence and their ambivalent attitude towards their role as women.

Conclusion

A great many things seem to happen in a group. People relax and reveal themselves more quickly than they usually do in one-to-one situations. In some cases there seems to be a conscious decision to communicate, in others it is as though the group acts as a sort of hotbed in which things develop and come to fruition which would probably never have germinated in a different setting. Group pressures are considerable and may at times seem too much for some members, but group support can be equally strong. The supporting, enabling, clarifying function in a group is not confined to the worker. It is shared by everyone.

4

Groupwork with children

Communication with children

Children find it difficult to put their anxieties, wishes and feelings into words even in the most favourable circumstances, and those with whom social workers come into contact are likely to have special difficulties. Many will come from homes where even the adult vocabulary is limited and speech adapted to practical purposes rather than to the exploration of feeling. In addition to this, they will not usually have experienced secure and loving family relationships, and are likely to be more than averagely disturbed, withdrawn or delinquent. Casework sessions with children are, therefore, likely to be stilted, with very little spontaneous communication from the child, particularly in the early stages. Even an experienced and skilled caseworker finds himself falling back on question and answer interviews and social chat about school and television. The child is only too likely to withdraw into his shell in what appears a threatening situation, adopting a stiff, polite 'say as little as possible' manner or actually refusing to speak. Many caseworkers employ some sort of play

37

activity to break the ice while still retaining the one-to-one situation. To some, playgroups have seemed the logical next step.

The leader's role

In playgroups taken by a social worker the group leader's role is permissive. His authority is not made explicit except in certain peripheral ways; for example, he insists on attendance and limits dangerous behaviour. There is no programme or planned activity of any kind, the children are not taught a game or hobby, and no one is given a task to do or a role to take. Play material is provided and the children decide what to do, and stop doing it whenever they wish. They need not do anything at all. In the early stages the worker might make a tentative suggestion to a shy child that, for example, he might like to paint, but that is all. If a group member wishes to spend an entire session or a series of sessions assembling and reassembling a jigsaw puzzle, or kicking a ball against the door with his back to the room, or dropping dead, he is free to do so. The worker is there to be related with, talked to and acted at, to be questioned and occasionally to interpret as the need arises. At times the atmosphere may be quiet and absorbed, and at others it is screaming thumping chaos with perhaps a ball game and puppet show trying to out-shout each other.

Practical considerations

The practical considerations in planning groups were listed in an earlier chapter, but a note on their application in this sort of group may be helpful. The room should be fairly small so that the group stays together, and it must be stripped of valuable and breakable objects. The fire should be screened and the light protected by some sort of paper or cloth shade rather than by a glass one. The window should be at least partially protected, perhaps by placing a large piece of equipment in front of it. If possible all furniture except a table and some chairs should be removed. Material must be provided for imaginative and self-expressive play bearing in mind the sex and age of the children. They are going to get very excited and the risk of injury is an important consideration in selecting the toys. Some things will be used by all children, a big light plastic ball, paper and paints, chalk and crayons. A puppet theatre can be constructed of three hinged hardboard boards with a stage cut in the centre panel, and hand puppets made of papier-mache and scraps of material. Apart from its original purpose the theatre will be used as a house, a hideout, a fort or a prison as the children play out their fantasies. Dressing up materials are used by either sex; for example, boys will use a selection of men's hats in their games. Toys are chosen which can be utilised in the expression of aggression without the risk of injury : toy guns without ammunition, rubber daggers and hammers. A few quieter games such as dominoes, draughts and cards provide an opportunity for withdrawal to more conventional 'adult' behaviour and also a chance to relate with the groupworker in a different way.

In this sort of hyperactive group numbers must be kept low, not more than six children being included. It is more difficult to listen and to follow what is happening in the constant noise and movement of a playgroup than in discussion group.

There will be absences and late arrivals, and this means

SWG—D

that at times a child will be alone with the groupworker. Children seem to welcome these occasional individual sessions and make the best use of the worker's private ear. The sort of children who are shy and inarticulate in a series of interviews treat the one-to-one situation differently when it occurs in a group project. This may be because they are more relaxed, but there would also appear to be an element of competition and rivalry. A boy who feels he needs this individual attention may contrive to arrive very early for several sessions. Occasionally, it may be necessary to arrange an individual interview with a child—for example, to discuss some practical problem which he and his parents would prefer to be kept private, but on the whole these 'private' sessions seem to weave naturally into the group experience and children will arrange this for themselves or can be asked to stay on afterwards.

Groups should, if possible, be held weekly so that they become part of the regular pattern of the child's life. They are intensive and exhausting for all concerned and an hour is generally felt to be long enough. Where possible the meetings should extend over a substantial period, say about a year or so, but short-term groups may be necessary in some circumstances. With regard to selection the general considerations listed earlier apply to play groups. In particular, it may be necessary to exclude a coldly sadistic child, but on the whole the group seems to be able to contain and exercise control over quite aggressive and violent children. Psychotic and very seriously disturbed children should not be included without psychiatric consultation and support. The general considerations also apply in deciding whether to run open or closed groups, although on the whole children seem less initially hostile to new group members than do adolescent and adult groups.

A boys' group

The group to be described here is of six boys aged 10-13 on probation or under supervision for non-attendance at school. The level of intelligence is around average, except for one boy who is quite illiterate and awaiting admission to an ESN school. The level of attainment at school is usually lower than the level of intelligence would warrant.

Such children are often from broken homes, and in this group only one child was living with both parents. They are frequently withdrawn and inarticulate and their truanting and petty delinquency, although a nuisance to society, may have a healthy motivation rooted in their desire to assert themselves, to attain status and friends and to escape in adventurous and exciting activity from the depressing realities of their family life, their failure at school and so on. To be caught and brought before the Court is part of the risk which makes the game exciting, and the amount of shame and anxiety it brings varies, although almost all children dread the idea of being removed from home. Their initial reaction to the probation officer is usually fear, which may be disguised as pseudo-adult indifference or that sort of submissive passive behaviour which is designed to let the child slip through without coming into conflict or indeed real contact of any kind with anyone in authority.

When groupwork was first tried in these circumstances the risk of contamination by association was often raised. It is a possibility which must be borne in mind in the selection of group members, but it is in many ways far less of a danger in the group situation than in the unavoidable unsupervised association which goes on all the time in waiting rooms and corridors, on the streets and in school. A Home Office report on groupwork in probation (Barr) found only one instance in 72 groups studied where meeting in a group *could* have been instrumental in members offending together.

When this group started the groupworker had recently returned to work after a long illness, was very weak and walking with a stick. Whether or not this affected the matter the boys, far from taking advantage of the permissive situation and behaving badly, expressing their agression and so on, were rather good and quiet, playing with the jigsaw and the draughts rather than the ball and the guns, teaching the groupworker to play dominoes and on one occasion even bringing a Mary Poppins game to play.

The psychiatrist who was advising on this project suggested that the boys hesitated to act out their aggression in the group for fear that this might bring control from the woman groupworker which would in turn be too great a threat to their emerging masculinity. At his suggestion a male colleague joined the group. This gave the group a father and an opportunity for masculine identification. This was particularly valuable because not one of the boys had lived in a stable and lifelong relationship with his real father.

The introduction of a male groupworker, although beneficial in the long run, produced initially a kind of shock, and the boys obviously resented him as a rival for the woman's attention, an only too large cuckoo in the nest. For several sessions he was pointedly ignored and the youngest and probably the most disturbed boy in the group, a lively ten-year old West Indian, who was

42

in the habit of drawing frequent pictures of witches clearly identifying these with the groupworker, for the first time drew a cat on the witch's broomstick. When asked what it was he said it was the witch's kitten, thus putting the intruder literally in his place.

The male worker decided to remain fairly quiet and inactive, and after a while the boys began to approach him and relate to him in various ways. At this point group activity began to grow markedly noisier and more masculine and aggressive as the boys strove to impress 'father', although they did not abandon the group norms already established about not injuring each other, damaging property and so on. Rather to the groupworkers' surprise an over-excited child, apparently quite unaware of their presence, would still stop and ask permission before he did anything which might be damaging (like chalk on the walls), or take a first tentative step in a new activity and wait for the groupworkers' approval, or at least lack of censure, before repeating it.

The boys tended to divide the group activities into two parts, establishing a sort of refuge of quiet play and talk round the table where the woman sat, and one of lively masculine activity in the rest of the room, involving the male worker more or less actively. The two centres, however, had plenty of intercommunication. Both were included in the talk that went on, and the male worker was asked from time to time to play dominoes, while the woman noticed that in the most violent and excited ball game a boy would glance over his shoulder to see if she had appreciated a specially skilful throw or kick. She would also notice that if she showed, however slightly, anxiety over some violently aggressive behaviour which might lead to real injury, the boy who was, say, appar-

43

ently gouging his opponent's eye out, would often pause to grin at her reassuringly.

In this situation it was important that the groupworkers should have good mutual understanding. As time passed they began to see what their respective roles were and gradually with practice and discussion worked as a team making spontaneous contributions to the life of the group, sharing interpretations and so on.

Children in such a group will commonly have experience of unstable family relationships and, following patterns which have evolved at home, may be motivated at an unconscious level to recreate these situations in the group by rivalry among themselves and attempting to manipulate the groupworkers and create dissention between them. Once relationships have been formed, these attempts can usefully be acknowledged and interpreted to the boys at a simple level.

The group atmosphere is disinhibitive, and the boys are permitted to express aggression not only against one another but against the groupworker verbally or in symbolic play. As previously mentioned this will usually, especially at first, be expressed indirectly and in generalised terms, and it is important that the boys should be encouraged by the workers' permissive attitude and by interpretation to be more direct so that the situation can be worked through and used.

One very disturbed boy in the group was proving quite unmanageable in his school. He boasted of his behaviour over a series of meetings, complained of frequent canings and expressed anger and contempt against his teachers. This repeated itself without change or improvement until the groupworker, who was in touch with the school, decided to put the reality situation to him and remarked

44

that if he went on like this he would inevitably be excluded from day school and sent to some sort of boarding school, sorry though she would be to lose him. He made no reply, but on the following week greeted her with a lively account of a row he had had with a prefect he had considered too bossy, ending with 'and so I kicked *her* in the stomach.' The worker's suggestion that perhaps he felt that on the previous week she had been a bit like the prefect and that he would have liked to kick her in the stomach met with a polite denial but a fiendish acknowledging grin.

After this he began to talk about his school experiences in a different way, showing real depression rather than bravado, and explaining that for various reasons he could never behave well so long as he went to that school. He elaborated this in subsequent discussions, showing some insight into his difficulties, and after a further crisis a change of school was eventually arranged. What seemed to have happened was that he was able to express against the groupworker, with whom he had a very positive relationship, his feelings of anger and resentment because she failed to appreciate his difficulties. He found that she understood and did not reject him, and so was able to discuss his troubles and their solution in a more mature way, and subsequently to seek and accept a change of school.

The expression of aggression may take the form of a physical attack on the groupworker, probably thinly disguised as an accident arising out of play activity. Policy as to how much of this is to be permitted will have to be decided bearing in mind the age and sex of the workers. At one school for maladjusted children in Sweden the psychiatrist-superintendent mentioned size as a prime consideration in selecting both male play therapists and dogs because they must be able to defend themselves without injuring small boys! Whatever general decision is reached on this point, it is essential that aggression, however symbolic or carefully disguised as accident should be acknowledged for what it is and, if appropriate, interpreted.

At first it may seem impossible to distinguish the contrived 'accident' from the genuine one, but after a while it is easy to make the distinction. For example, one notices that two or three boys can play ball violently on one side of a small room without the ball hitting the groupworker, with dramatic 'saves' skilfully practised. If at one session the ball strikes the worker or the activity in which she is engaged, rather frequently, this is an expression of aggression and should be acknowledged as such.

On one such occasion the aggressor was a withdrawn, educationally subnormal boy, normally quiet, a skilful ball-player who was well able to control the ball's direction. On this occasion he was playing by himself as he often did, and the ball fell on the table where the groupworker was playing dominoes with two other children, or struck her, two or three times. The groupworker's comment that he seemed to be annoyed with her was met with smiling denial, but he volunteered the opinion that dominoes was a girl's game. The groupworker's reply that she had thought it commonly played by men was ignored. It later emerged that this boy, who was completely illiterate, was identifying all activities connected with reading, writing and counting as effeminate. With a little encouragement he developed his theme. Driving a lorry and working in a garage (his father's and brother's occupations respectively) were highly praised, and he boasted of his own understanding of these matters and, expanding visibly,

46

spoke of week-ends helping them with a moving van, referring to his pocket-money as beer-money. He expressed a preference for films about monsters and strong men like Samson, and his intention of joining a weight-lifting class.

At the same time he concealed, with a great deal of determination, the fact that he could not read, and responded to the groupworker's suggestion that lorry-drivers needed to be able to read road signs by saying that the signs were stupid and misleading, and it was better to ask the way. This 12-year old child, still attending a secondary modern school where he could have understood very little of what was going on, had found a way of making his failure tolerable to himself.

In arranging the transfer to a special school, which he and his family had previously resisted, the worker was careful to stress the superior instruction in practical subjects available, and to involve the boy's admired father in all negotiations.

The risk of aggression causing injury to the groupworker is slight, but the risk of the boys injuring one another is present to a greater or less extent according to the degree of disturbance and the history of violent behaviour among the members. Steps must be taken to avoid injury on the lines suggested earlier in this chapter, but the greatest safety precaution is the attentive presence of the groupworker, and he should so arrange things that he is free from interruption during group sessions.

Excited children, tired of throwing the ball at each other, may seize a heavier object—for example, a lump of plasticine for the purpose, or, the supply of rubber daggers having run out, arm themselves with wooden-handled paint brushes. The worker's calm comment 'that could really hurt someone, give it to me', re-enforces the group norms. In fact the boys know the difference between acted and real aggression perfectly well, and if the worker fails to observe a danger someone will quite probably draw his attention to it. Most boys seem to work up to and through a crescendo of violent behaviour and then adopt a more adult role and a more mature relationship with the groupworkers. It may be difficult at first to distinguish an individual's crescendo from one which involves the whole group because the others will join in his pattern of play, but after a time it becomes clear who is the centre of this particular drama and who are supporting players. Boys who have been through their own crescendo of aggression in the group tend to play the part of an older brother, also engaging the groupworkers in more adult games and conversation and so on.

Self appointed leaders arise in the group. Some boys never seek the role, others occupy it for a long period while some slip in and out of the position several times. Would-be leaders play their parts with varying degrees of tact. If they prove unacceptable their efforts at leadership are ignored by the group almost as if they were invisible and inaudible. There are many kinds of member-leader. The two most common are the boy who leads the activity, at least for a time suggesting the games, heightening the tension and excitement, leading the group into more aggressive channels of behaviour; and the one who tries to take charge, introduce more organised games with rules and generally control the group in a more conventional and rigid way than the permissive groupworker, although at times he may attempt a quite shrewd imitation of his methods.

One objection sometimes raised to this kind of groupwork with children is that it does nothing to discipline them. This is certainly true if one thinks of discipline in the narrow, parade-ground sense of the word. However, the Oxford Dictionary of Etymology gives 'chastisement, penitential correction' as the meaning of the word in the 13th century only; by the 16th century it had already come to mean 'a system of control over conduct'. What the group seems to encourage is in fact a kind of self-discipline, and this already has an odd, old-fashioned 19th century sound. Many children in need of a social worker's care come from homes where the discipline if any is as practised in the 13th century, and there are schools where in overcrowded low-stream classes this is still, however regretfully, the last resort, so the group discipline, which is not unlike that of a good family, may be a new experience for them.

Children are surprisingly good at assessing the group situation and accepting it, and the peripheral rules often do not need to be explicitly stated. A game of ball may develop into something between a wrestling match and the Eton Wall Game, or a handball game be devised in which the goal is one's opponent's face, but no-one really gets hurt. On one occasion when a new boy, misjudging the situation, started a real fight, the group saw what was happening before the worker did and moved as one man to bring the situation under control.

Children do not need to be told that the group is a special place and that the uninhibited behaviour permitted there would not be allowed in the building generally. Of course, they will try out the situation from time to time, usually not repeating any particular test more than once. For example, a boy may open a door and kick the ball into the passage, coming in at once when the worker says

49

'only in the room'. If the worker ignores a new departure, as for example, standing on the chairs, the boys will probably ask directly 'May we stand on the chairs?'

One particular pattern of damage and reparation developed into a ritual. One wall of the room was made of old plaster and broke very easily. The first time this happened the boys suspended the game, appeared apprehensive and waited to see what the groupworkers would do. They remarked that the wall was defective and suggested a change of positions so that the wooden door became the target. A few weeks later the ball hit the wall again accidentally and another piece of plaster broke off. The groupworker fetched some gummed labels to make a temporary repair and all the boys abandoned their game to help him. After that the illiterate boy referred to earlier took over the task and the others suspended their game whenever necessary, without protest, so that he could repair the wall, which he did with care and evident satisfaction.

In a playgroup the boys can experience an atmosphere not unlike that of a good family, which is re-educative in itself. They understand and observe those group norms best which they have worked out for themselves. When they test any aspect of the situation it is abundantly obvious that they are testing and not defying, and the tester-out will receive comments from the group, as well as interpretations from the leader, on his behaviour. A 12-year-old who constantly threw things about the room, staggered about and talked nonsense might pretend not to understand when the groupworker asked him how old he was now? but the others shouted good-naturedly '2! He's 2!'

Children seem to take very naturally to the situation, to like it and respond to it. Although they seldom sit down and talk quietly for long, they talk to one another and the groupworkers all the time they are playing, often about things which are important and emotionally loaded. In some ways they are less leader-centred than some adolescent and adult groups, and a boy's account of a fight, trouble at home or school, or an outing of some kind will be supplemented by the experiences of others and, if appropriate, by frank and amiable comment on the speaker's veracity. They have to share the workers with other children, but the relationship seems to have more rather than less depth because of this, and both sides become more real to each other. The worker's affection for the children is engaged, but at the same time they are able to see very clearly the problems they are likely to present at home and school.

5

The group in an institution

General considerations

A social worker considering groupwork in a residential setting faces most of the considerations previously described, and also a new and complex set of circumstances. He is certainly not working in a vacuum, but in a group within a group, an island of purposive small group experience in the sea of institutional relationships. Interaction in the institution is more concentrated and intense altogether than that in the outside world which surrounds the group taken in the social worker's office, described in the previous chapter. Members of the latter kind of group may not know one another outside. Even if they are acquainted as neighbours or at school or work they are not living together as are members of institutional groups, who are, however partially and temporarily, cut off from the outside world. They are in close interaction with their companions and the staff, projecting onto them patterns of earlier relationships. Residential staff carry a heavy burden, and it is the social worker's function to be supportive rather than destructive. He may have to face the fact that he cannot support a particular institutional regime and that, if he cannot modify it, it might be better if he worked elsewhere. On the other hand, he may be lucky enough to work in, or in connection with, a progressive institution where he can learn a great deal. Between these two extremes lies a range of institutions where with patience and goodwill on both sides the social worker can conduct a group in a way useful to the group members and also to the institution. Such groups, however, will always present special difficulties and be unusually complex in their dynamics.

The life of the institution flows in and out of the group in a disconcerting way. The groupworker may be the only person present who does not know what is going on outside the group; for example that two of the members quarrelled that morning, that another is upset because she has had no letters from home, or that a fourth is in violent conflict with a staff member. Remembering that a group is a microcosm of life in general and that members of a social worker's groups are likely to be more delinquent, disturbed and/or neurotic than usual, it should not surprise the worker to discover that members of the group will try to involve him in their conflict with authority generally, and with individual members of staff, and that some can do this subtly and cleverly. They may invite the groupworker to comment on some apparently theoretical or neutral situation which is, unknown to him, a real source of trouble. Anything he says about it, however innocent, may be carried back into the institution and there repeated 'with advantages' causing anxiety and annoyance to the staff and possibly increasing rather than otherwise the group members' sense of insecurity and unreality.

53

If the staff of a residential institution has the same sort of training and general background as the groupworker, a good basis exists for mutual understanding, although goodwill and tolerance will still be needed on both sides. If their professional training is different but their aims roughly the same, as, for example, in the case of well-qualified nurses in a progressive psychiatric unit, mutual understanding and respect can be reached. However, if the institution is staffed by workers whose concept of their role is mainly that of benevolent control, then there are difficulties which may be insuperable. Of course, these difficulties would also face anyone doing casework in an institution, but groupwork, because it is somehow more pervasive, is particularly threatening to a rigid organisation. Faced with this situation, a groupworker should think carefully before deciding to do groupwork in an institution. The staff may be functioning adequately in their own way and be too set in that way, or too insecure, to face change. The sort of permissive, non-directive group described in this study, operating in an establishment so staffed, could destroy more than it created.

A group in a probation hostel

The description which follows is based on the experience of a woman probation officer, over a number of years, in taking discussion groups of adolescent girls in a probation hostel.

Probation hostels receive young people between the ages of 15 and 21 in whose cases a Court has made a probation or supervision order with a condition of residence for not longer than twelve months. They are exposed to the good influence of the staff, provided with a reasonably disciplined regime of life, expected to work regularly and so on. Anyone who is the subject of such an order may be sent to a probation hostel, but the Courts are more likely to take this course with those who have more than usually severe behaviour problems or less than usually supportive homes.

A good relationship between the warden and the probation officer, important if residents are to be helped in anything more than a superficial way, becomes crucial if groupwork is attempted.

Young girls who have been brought before the court as being in moral danger form a substantial proportion of those in a probation hostel. Others may be on probation for stealing, often from shops or from other women's purses or handbags. Whatever the original reason for the court appearance, the decision to remove them from home to a probation hostel is usually based on both the young person's behaviour and on the fact that the home is unhappy or the parents quite unable to cope with them. The girls have consented to a condition of residence in the probation order; some no doubt because they fear being sent to an approved school if they refuse, but many because they are genuinely depressed and restless. Apart from their own special difficulties, they present the behaviour problems normal to their age.

Communication with adolescents is by no means as difficult as it is with children. This is the talking time of life, and once any sort of trust is developed, adolescents will usually speak fairly freely in the one-to-one situation, although they tend to avoid—as we all do—really painful subjects unless under strain or at a period of crisis. It is also the time when their own age-group is all-important to them, and setting an adolescent in a group is providing a natural habitat, and incidentally giving them a chance to discover by interaction, comparison and experiment their own individuality. They listen to and talk with one another, and, supported by their peers, are likely to open out rather more on the ambivalent feelings towards adults and 'their' society which are natural to this age-group.

The groups to be described have been held at intervals over a period of ten years, and various methods of handling the situation have been tried. The practical considerations involved in this kind of group are listed in the order they are presented in Chapter 2.

Meetings were held on the hostel premises, and different rooms were used for different groups, as chance and general convenience dictated. The least relaxing setting was probably the formal reception room furnished with a large polished table and chairs which the girls normally only visit briefly. The office was used on one occasion, but this was next to the chapel so that loud talk and laughter had to be discouraged. At other times the group met in a small work-room. A comfortably furnished sitting room was used and also the more barely furnished recreation room where the girls normally play records, dance and so on. On the whole, it was felt that the more familiar and less formal the room the better.

The right number for such a group seemed to be about 7, although numbers from 4 to 12 were experimented with. Seven is enough for a choice of roles and interaction and not too many for mutual attention and comprehension.

Weekly meetings were considered ideal, but proved impractical for most of the time owing to other pressures on the groupworker. Groups usually met fortnightly, and even then there were unavoidable interruptions owing to emergencies, and to leave and sickness. As an experiment, groups were held once a month in one series, but the long interval seemed to destroy all continuity. After some experimentation the sessions were timed for one hour, and it seemed better to keep fairly firmly to the time stated. The population of a hostel is always changing and it is difficult to generalise about how many group meetings any girl might attend. The groups were never long-term and between 6 and 12 meetings over 2-4 months would be about average.

Various methods of selection were tried particularly in the early stages. As in all new projects it was tempting to fill the group with the most difficult girls, who were behaving badly in the hostel and/or were withdrawn and unresponsive in the one-to-one situation. This method loads the scales heavily against the inexperienced group-worker and was abandoned in favour of selecting, in consultation with the warden, a mixed group which deliberately included some outgoing people likely to respond easily to the group situation and others in need of special encouragement and help.

In one series—an open group—the girls were allowed to select new members themselves which led to the concentration in the group of the most delinquent girls in the hostel! After a while, the practice of including the girls in the group in the order of their arrival in the hostel was adopted, thus providing unselected mixed groups.

The groups have mainly been closed, that is they have started and finished with the same girls, drop-outs not being replaced. Open groups were tried from time to time. Although the newcomers were fellow-residents the group seemed to resent their inclusion and the new girl

57

stayed apart from the group at least for a time. In short-term groups this is a serious disadvantage.

The probation officer acting as group leader saw the girls individually about every two weeks. In these interviews a very simple explanation of the purpose of the group was given along the lines that 'You have probably heard from the other girls that I sometimes see them together in a group. We get to know each other better and some people find it easier to talk there. We can talk about anything you like to bring up and often find that the girls can understand and help each other'. Girls were then asked if they wanted to ask any questions about the group, and whether they were willing to join. Occasionally a girl was reluctant, and was not pressed. Before the group, the worker memorised some details of the case history, family position and present troubles of the members.

After some experimentation it was decided not to raise the question of confidentiality specifically in the group. There was no way of guaranteeing it as group members would have friends and confidantes in the institution who were not in the group. The worker, too, had responsibilities and loyalties outside the group, to the warden, to society and to the court, and the members understood this. Perhaps because of the decision to accept this realistically, the question of confidentiality, which had loomed large in group planning, did not seem so crucial in practice.

The worker saw the girls individually before the group started, while it was running and after it finished. Some writers on groupwork insist that the worker should have no contact with members outside the group. This is a reasonable stand for a psychiatrist to take, and if necessary he can call on the patient's G.P. or on a psychiatric

58

social worker attached to his unit for assistance; but a social worker normally works alone and is very much involved in his client's life generally. In many settings he has both authority over him and practical obligations towards him. In this setting, for example, it would be quite unreasonable and inhumane not to allow a girl to discuss in private matters which she wished kept private but about which she required help. For example, she might fear her stepfather's continued sexual assault and so be reluctant to return home. Similarly, it would be unreasonable to compel her to take part in the group in the sort of discussion and assessment of serious misbehaviour which may lead to her reappearance in court. When a girl herself brings these matters up in the group it is a different matter, but it is important that she should have a choice. A very shy and withdrawn girl will sometimes listen in silence to another talking about her difficulties, for example, with her father, and at her next individual session begin to talk for the first time about her family situation, freely and with obvious relief. A social worker must at times be both groupworker and caseworker to the client and a realistic acceptance of this fact may be followed by the discovery that one situation can 'feed' the other.

In this particular group the authority inherent in group leadership is reinforced by the members' circumstances. The leader is a probation officer, and they can observe and will sometimes test out the good working relationship which exists between her and the warden. Group members react to this situation differently according to their personalities, their experience of similar relationships and their relative maturity. Response can range from overdependence to a very attacking aggression. Allowing for all the other factors, age has significance. Adolescence sometimes looks like a second weaning, and young adolescents are more likely to be dependent and clinging, while older ones wish to assert their independence. The situation is trebly loaded—adolescence, delinquency and the institutional setting.

Members react to the group experience and the leader's permissive attitude in some cases with strong hostility, although without encouragement it will usually be considered too dangerous to direct openly against the groupworker. Instead other adults in authority will be criticised, the police, teachers, adults generally and finally their parents. The leader's response is all-important. She must bring into the open and acknowledge that some at least of this hostility is being directed against her, and must neither be stung into retaliation nor collapse and be destroyed. At times the attack may feel very damaging but, like the egg-shaped weighted toys given to small children, the groupworker must roll back into an upright position however often she is pushed over. It helps to realise that, as in the case of the tutor described in the next chapter, this expression of hostility is directed at the groupworker not mainly because of anything she really is or has done, but because the group pressures have triggered off a pattern of response formed in earlier life. To work through this with someone who is not going to respond to hostility with hostility can be a corrective experience, and this, with a measure of insight, can help the girls to cope with such situations better in the future. It must be remembered that aggression is revealed but not created by the group situation and that it tends to be covered and concealed, rather than utilised by ordinary methods of discipline.

In the group the girls sometimes felt able to express freely their anger or resentment, their fear of being unloved and, usually less directly, their feelings of guilt. It was not only that they could sometimes put into words something that they felt deeply, but that these feelings were understood, accepted and shared by others. They talked about their childhood, giving full rein to depression and anger over parental rejection, although this was sometimes expressed elliptically. On one occasion a girl who was her mother's eldest, and only illegitimate, daughter and had always been rejected by her stepfather, told the group that she had seen him seize a baby sister, who was club-footed, and throw her against the kitchen door, saying that the child was none of his. (It was true that the crippled child had to be removed from home because of the father's ill-treatment.) The group shared the shock, and the mourning, appropriate to such inhumanity. The groupworker, although aware of some of the underlying factors, felt that generally speaking, she could only deal with what the girls themselves brought out in the group and that it was therefore inappropriate (as it would in any case have been superfluous) to say 'and that is how you feel he has treated you, because although you haven't a club-foot, you are illegitimate.'

Neither could she bring up in the group a matter which the girl was discussing freely in the individual sessions—her pregnancy and fear that the father of the child, with whom she had a longstanding relationship, was not going to marry her. This fear of another rejection probably helped to spark off her outburst in the group.

The girls talked about recent events, the trouble which had brought them to the hostel, their parents' quarrels and, over and over again, about the feeling of being unwanted and rejected by one or both parents. The minority who had a happier experience tended to keep quiet at this stage, at most saying very quietly, 'My mother wasn't like that at all'. Those with grievances would, allowed free expression, sometimes 'talk themselves round' and begin to express more positive feelings and bring out their parents' good points, or excuse their behaviour. 'My dad was a good worker though, not like some.' 'Mind you, my mum has terrible heads, they made her real bad,' as if having expressed anger they felt to be punishing they were experiencing remorse and a desire to forgive.

They also discussed the hostel, their community life, and its difficulties. Quarrels and grievances were aired in the group. On one occasion a West Indian girl struck an Irish one just before the group started. She sat curled in an armchair in silence, like a young tiger ready to spring, while the other girls told her that they really did like her and that she was too touchy and quick to take offence. She accepted this with a grin, and an assurance that she didn't mean anything either when she called them white bastards. They then began to unravel the pattern of events which had led to the blow and it became patently obvious that a third member of the group had provoked the quarrel. The focus of the group then swung to this third girl, who had a great deal of open hostility to the world in general and to her elderly adoptive parents in particular. She was silent and showed no emotion except cool amusement, and did not respond to the worker's suggestion that she might like to give her version of what had happened. It was felt that she in fact derived little benefit from the incident, but the group perceived clearly and discussed with interest, and in a relatively relaxed way, both the event and something of their pattern of inter-relationship in the group and in the institution.

When this sort of thing happened the groupworker

asked questions aimed at clarifying the picture, encouraged members to give their opinions and, very occasionally and as circumstances demanded, spoke firmly and with authority about her attitude to certain kinds of behaviour, saying for example that bullying and physical ill-treatment of one girl by another would not be tolerated either by hostel staff or by herself. She did not use her authority to control what happened in the group: she permitted noisy, aggressive and rude behaviour to go unchecked as far as she was concerned, although very often group members would attempt to check it. This attitude was easier to maintain in a small group of 5-7. If more girls were present this sort of behaviour seemed to lead to the group disintegrating temporarily into couples and groups of three with little intercommunication.

It was interesting to see that girls who found it safe to express aggression and even quite personal hostility to the worker in the special group situation seldom carried this over into individual interviews. Some obviously felt it too dangerous to contemplate and feared reprisals now that they no longer had the backing of their peers. The more intelligent and mature girls, if asked, would explain patiently that, of course, they had not really meant it personally, and show surprise that the worker had not understood that. They were fed up because, for example, they were worried about the future, or they knew their fathers had no love for them, and so on. It usually emerged, however, that the worker herself was sometimes seen as at fault in these situations. She was too controlling because she did not approve of some plan they had made, or really useless because she could not in some way make things all right at home, or a potential danger because she wanted them to think of things they would rather forget. So the hostility was in a way really directed against her, on whom they had projected their dissatisfaction with adult authority in general and with their parents in particular.

It is the fear that emotion in general and aggression in particular may, in some mysterious way, get out of hand, that helps to discourage some caseworkers from using groupwork. The group does exert its own pressures, emotions can run high and behaviour may be less circumspect. Most groupworkers find the experience, however fascinating, very tiring indeed, and it is as well to time the group session so that it is followed by a rest or a meal. In practice, however, things do seem to stop short of panic and havoc, and groups do seem to have some sort of built-in self-regulating mechanism. Actual violence is unlikely, and if it should occur will be controlled by group members. Individuals in the group do not all reach a peak of tension and self-expression at once. The expression, face to face, of anger with a person in authority, and the experience of having that anger courteously accepted, does not seem to produce a lack of respect—quite the reverse.

6

Groups in social work education

This chapter comments on the operation, in groups which form part of social work education, of the sort of pressures and interactions described elsewhere in the study. It is not intended as a study of social work education in general. Of the many kinds of groups in operation some of the most common are:

(a) Groups which are part of full-time training courses for beginners, advanced students or trained and/or experienced social workers;

(b) those arranged by an agency for its own staff as part of an in-service training scheme;

(c) groups arranged by some outside body, for example university, clinic, or professional society and attended by social workers from one or a number of agencies.

The material most commonly used as a basis for group discussion is an account of a case known to one of the students, presented by him and discussed by the group then and in subsequent sessions if required. Other students ask questions about the case history and about current problems, make tentative diagnoses, suggest how the case might be handled and give their opinions as to likely future developments. All this is discussed freely between the students and the tutor. Another method is to use a general subject as a basis for discussion : compiling a case history, the home visit, working with the mentally ill, the use of interpretation, authority in casework and so on. It is sometimes felt that this sort of discussion is undesirable unless it is centred round a case so that the group keeps firmly to reality. However, it can, with good leadership, help students to think clearly about the principles they are applying.

The tutor may be a specially-qualified social worker teaching full or part-time, or someone from another discipline, most commonly from psychiatry. In in-service training he may be a member of the agency's staff. The qualifications and training of the tutor, and his personality, affect the way he will conduct the group, the student's expectations of him and the use they make of 'his' group. The group content is also affected by the quality of the students, so that no two groups are alike. The tutor's function is to foster the group's capacity for mutual clarification and support and to keep the group broadly to its task.

Students may also be helped to relate theory to practice, to understand the content of specialised lectures and to see their application in the field.

A students' discussion group does not follow the conventional pattern set by a lecture followed by questions and discussion, neither is it the decision-making group of management training. It is task-oriented to the learning of casework methods. Problems are discussed and solutions canvassed, but it is rare that a decision has to be made. The group tutor assists in the pooling and clarifica-
66

tion of knowledge already available in the group, rather than listing facts, describing theories or advising on procedure, although he may do all of these on occasions.

Learning in groups is affected by relationships between the students as well as by those they form with the tutor. Theoretically this makes good selection important, but in practice very little choice may be possible. If the group is to be of short duration it will probably have more chance of clear communication and mutual understanding if it is reasonably homogeneous, consisting of people of a roughly similar level of education and experience. However, a mixed group is likely to be more stimulating, and a wide range of training and experience can usefully be combined provided that the group has time to settle down, sort itself out and find a common language. The one thing that appears to create difficulty is the inclusion of people with a total lack of experience. It then becomes rather like trying to teach rock-climbing to the inhabitants of a completely flat country. If they have never encountered the difficulties they are unlikely to appreciate the value of the techniques.

Students new to social work need to adjust the concept of the tutor-teacher role they formed during their schooldays, which has been more or less confirmed by the programme of formal lectures which are included in their course. This is that the tutor will provide facts which can be assimilated intellectually and reproduced later in an examination. Casework learning, which involves feeling as well as thinking, is likely to be disturbing, and students will try to learn it by means to which they are accustomed, so that, particularly to begin with, discussion may take the form of reproducing learned theories and formulating intricate psychoanalytic diagnoses rather than considering the realities of the case under discussion. When the tutor declines to provide an authoritative ruling along these or any other lines the group's preferred solution may be referral to some specialised, probably psychiatric, agency on the grounds that someone, somewhere, must know the right answer. Denied their habitual defence against the threat of new learning, that of paying lip-service to the tutor's superior knowledge while secretly believing that what he says is impractical, the student is forced to contribute from his own experience and understanding and so, hopefully, to begin to learn.

Most students have experienced some form of competition in their school life and in the group, too, they would like to be 'top of the class'. They know that, however permissive the group situation, there will be some sort of recognition of success at the end of the course. Communications, therefore, may be designed to placate, please or impress the tutor rather than to extend the student's understanding. This desire to succeed may impede his willingness to describe frankly his actual behaviour towards his clients and to accept the feelings that the latter arouse in him because of the sometimes justified fear that giving voice to them may bring down disapproval from the other students and from the tutor.

While all this is going on the tutor is under great pressure to assume omniscience. He is questioned and deferred to on matters of fact and on psychological and sociological theories, and it is sometimes difficult to distinguish legitimate requests for information from avoidance of the effort required to learn and grow. The tutor can help by accepting the student's anxiety and generalising about his feelings in a way which shows that they are considered normal and shared by others including the tutor himself. 'What does the group feel that this client is doing to make us all feel so rejecting?' or 'It is sometimes difficult, for all of us, to face and recognise a client's feelings and anxieties when they relate to something we ourselves have felt.'

Students' groups have a function distinct from that of therapeutic groups, in that they will discuss the problems of the person with whom the member is working and not, as in a therapeutic group, those of the members themselves. It is a part of the tutor's function to make this clear. However, a group is a group for whatever reason it has been called together. The group pressures and interactions described in previous chapters operate in training groups and, therefore, the dividing line between training and therapy will not always be clear. Social workers, sophisticated enough to recognise what is happening, will mostly guide themselves and keep the group to its learning task, but this is not true of untrained and inexperienced students. Their reaction to the group situation and to the emotional nature of the discussion material may be to turn from their clients' problems to their own.

The tutor can set the tone of the group from the beginning by directing all comments and interpretations to the case being presented and not to the person presenting. For example, if the student says 'I feel very angry with this woman', the tutor would not respond with 'Perhaps she reminds you of someone in your own past to whom you have hostile feelings', but with something along the lines of 'Is she perhaps deliberately provoking your anger—could she be repeating a pattern from her past in which she invites rejection and punishment, perhaps something to do with her relationship with her father?' etc. This makes the point, but focuses it on the case. The tutor may at times have to see good opportunities for interpretation and clarification pass without comment because the material on which they would be based was too personal to the student. Sometimes a simple generalised comment addressed to the group as a whole may be helpful, 'People sometimes feel that' or 'Most people are afraid of . . .'. Students will from time to time hear discussed in relation to their cases problems very near to their own, and, if they are able to relate one to the other, they may make progress towards self-understanding.

In students' groups patterns of reaction emerge similar to those which occur in therapeutic groups, but adapted to the learning situation. Students will from time to time appoint themselves as rival tutors, with varying amounts of support from the group, and behave in a way hostile or supportive, even protective to the tutor. Others may cast themselves for the role of his 'favourite pupil'. From time to time, training groups may produce students who fulfil other roles, as for example that of scapegoat.

The general comments on the handling of the 'scapegoat' situation described in Chapter Three apply in a teaching group. The tutor should not be too quick to intervene; the 'scapegoat' is frequently self-presenting and the situation may be worked through with benefit to himself and to the group. Only if he is persistently diverting the group from the theme being discussed or becoming stressed to an extent which may be damaging, should the group be given help in clarifying the situation—e.g. is the group using X as a recipient of the hostility they cannot bring themselves to express towards the tutor? Is X showing an attitude towards the client which the group inwardly shares and of which they are ashamed, or which they think the tutor may not approve?

70

Some of the anxiety, depression and resistance produced by the new ideas to which the students are being introduced and by the intensely emotional nature of the material being discussed is transferred to the group tutor. He is thought to be unable, or unwilling, to give them *everything* they want, which is always true, and of being particularly interested in some students or actually hostile to others, which may be true from time to time. These reactions will be more or less obvious in proportion to the general strain of the students' situation, and they tend to be more manifest and recognisable in the group than in individual tutorials because of the group pressures described elsewhere in this study. The experience may be exhausting and even painful to the tutor but, like other group leaders, he must cultivate indestructability. The hostility to which he is exposed is part of the students' learning process and fulfils a valuable purpose as far as they are concerned. It is part of the tutor's function to endure it. The tutor finds from experience that these feelings will be worked through and later seen by the student for what they were—part of a projective fantasy rather than a real-life experience. The tutor may at other times receive admiration and gratitude, even affection, out of all proportion to his deserts. In fact he will be the recipient from different students and from the same student at different times of attitudes of love and hate derived from their earlier life experience as well as from their present situation.

There is an additional difficulty in that the group is probably not the only contact between the tutor and the student. In an in-service group he may be a colleague, perhaps a senior one, and in a more academic setting he will certainly be seen as someone with the power to affect the student's success or failure on the whole course. Open expression of hostility, often helpful in the permissive atmosphere of the group, may be seen as a threat to the established pattern of good manners and staff relationships which exist and form a useful framework outside the group. In some cases, therefore, it might be better once again for the tutor to offer generalised comment rather than respond to individual aggression. For example: 'Is part of the trouble here that you (the group) are annoyed because you feel that there is a clear cut answer on this point which I *could* give you if I chose to do so? You are wrong about that, because there is no such answer. The factors which affect a person's development are infinitely complex and the nuances of interpersonal relationships delicate and shifting. In any situation the caseworker must operate on a sort of enlightened flexible guesswork, always ready to change his mind. He must learn to accept his own unawareness . . .'

The group pressures and the operation of group dynamics in such a group become very obvious from time to time. Once again, the border between education and therapy becomes confused. For example, a student with unresolved adolescent problems and therefore a strong general need to assert his independence of any kind of authority may display repeatedly and clearly, in the course of the group's life, his need to denigrate or hold up to ridicule the tutor or other lecturers. At the same time he may speak strongly in favour of stern disciplinary methods against the adolescent whose case is being discussed because he swears at or defies adults. In a therapeutic group the leader might, with the help of the group, encourage him to see in what way he is identifying with the person under discussion and displaying a wish to be punished and controlled. The group worker could do this either by interpretation or simply by allowing the situation to develop and repeat itself until the person himself saw what was happening. In a students' group however, the tutor may more appropriately focus the group's attention on the client being discussed and encourage them to explore his life history and present problems, to think about the background of an adolescent's anti-authority feelings, and to consider how he may be helped to understand them and to grow to maturity.

There is another kind of student whose reaction may be to offer material more appropriate to a therapeutic group. They may have serious difficulties in a general way, or just be under some special strain at the time. For example, a social worker without theoretical training in a group discussing anxiety in childhood, might suddenly present a childhood fantasy of her own of not being a real child and of never having to grow up and relate this to her present inability to accept the fact of middle age. The expression of this rejection of the fact of maturation (which involves acceptance of the consequent inevitability of death) could be a useful break-through in a therapeutic situation, but all the student can hope for in a group is the friendly attention of other students and the tutor, followed by return to the problems of the child whose case is under discussion. If more than this is needed then the tutor must decide at his discretion whether to try to help the student further, outside the group, or to refer her for psychiatric help. The difficulty here is that if the tutor becomes too involved in the student's personal problems he may no longer be able to fulfil his primary role of tutor. Students may legitimately hope to obtain clarification of and support in their professional role, insight

73

into human problems and, perhaps most valuable of all, the realisation that the social worker and the troubled person in need of help are, like the Colonel's lady and Judy O'Grady, sisters under the skin.

Hostility is not always directed against the tutor but may be focused on other students. Social workers and students are hopefully a relatively well-adjusted and mature set of people, and this sort of thing can usually be worked through without damage and indeed with some increase of self-knowledge on the part of the attacking person and the attacked. However, very occasionally under the group pressures a student will emerge who takes a consistently destructive role. Sometimes, especially with unsophisticated students, the concept of interpretation is seized on and misused as a weapon of assault rather than a helping tool. For example a male student may say to another 'Don't you think John that it is your client's homosexuality which makes you so anxious?' with the heavily significant implication that John himself had homosexual tendencies, latent or otherwise. The tutor can support the person so attacked, rather than attack the attacker, in general terms. A matter-of-fact contribution by him on the subject of homosexuality in general, its presence, however latent, in all of us, and our consequent reaction of fear and distaste when we meet it in our work will clarify the situation for the group and effectively neutralise the suggestion that John has special difficulties which are affecting his work adversely.

As the group progresses the tutor will find that communication is less leader-centred and that there is more interplay between the students. He can watch the group progress and intervene to help it along rather than being constantly peppered with questions as in the more aggres-

74

sive early stages. He and his group achieve some sort of corporate life as the students gain confidence and feel more accepted. The tutor is a stable figure who can help the group to work through their learning difficulties. He is not omniscient, but it is recognised that he knows more than the group does about the matter in hand and he understands most of the things they are trying to communicate and some of the anxieties they are experiencing. Later in the course the students may accept the tutor as neither a person possessing special magic nor a fake, but as someone who understands and can face the anxieties aroused in them by their realisation that neither they nor anyone else has professional omnipotence.

In social work education at present, groups are normally used to help to train students as caseworkers, and the material in this chapter is based on this assumption. Groups are, of course, also used in training social group-workers, and various methods have been tried of which two of the most common are:

1. Groups of social workers meeting with a tutor to discuss the notes of group sessions in which they acted as groupworker on the model of casework discussion groups.
2. Projects designed to give the members an opportunity to experience group dynamics directly in an intensive group situation. Some references are to be found in the final chapter, but the writers feel that there is not yet sufficient experience of these and other methods in the training of social groupworkers to make valid comment at this stage.

7

Theory and practice

Providing social workers with training and experience in group work may encourage them to hold more groups of their own. It will also have a beneficial effect upon all aspects of their work, in the form of an improved perception of the nature of interpersonal relationships. It becomes apparent that the individual is not a mere container for internal psychological processes, but a person in a social situation whose behaviour is largely determined by his past and present group memberships. Attention to what happens *between* people rather than *within* individuals is capable of wide application to, for instance, marital counselling and family casework.

Through experience in groups, workers, like clients, gain a more realistic conception of authority, an appreciation of the extent and limitations of individual autonomy and interdependence, an improved ability to communicate and to accept the differences between persons, and a clearer understanding of their own attitudes and feelings and the effects of their actions upon others. The gap between worker and client tends to diminish, and relationships are often, paradoxically, closer and more intense in the group than in the one-to-one situation.

Social work knowledge derives from psychology and sociology, but casework literature is often tediously platitudinous or anecdotal because this source knowledge is either not cited and treated as 'given', or used out of context, tentative hypotheses being given the status of received truths. The complex relationships between psychological and sociological frameworks of analysis are difficult to understand, resulting in neglect of wider aspects of the individual's problems. Perhaps the study and practice of groupwork may provide a means of assimilating broader frames of reference, and of adopting a more social focus for social work. The conventional juxtaposition of 'client' and 'society' involves units of such a different order and size, that the one becomes unpredictable, the other amorphous, and no convincing guide to social action is provided. The aim of 'adjustment' then seems to imply an acceptance of conventional values and a potential threat to the client's individuality. Directing helping efforts towards the client's social groups, large and small, would seem to provide a more realistic approach with a greater potential, allowing the client himself to strike a balance between accepting reality and attempting to change it.

Since the relevant literature is not particularly well known among social workers at present, this chapter provides brief résumés, inevitably entailing some distortion and omission, of the ideas of some important writers in this field. The basis for selection is their likely usefulness in groups run by social workers.

Psychoanalytic theories

Five psychoanalytic approaches to group treatment are

77

described. The work of Foulkes and of Bion would seem to have the greatest potential for development.

In the original works the person holding the group is referred to as 'therapist', 'conductor', 'analyst', 'leader' or 'doctor', and these words sometimes connote important theoretical differences. Nevertheless for the sake of clarity we have used 'therapist' throughout. Some of the differences between the writers may be clarified if the following considerations are borne in mind:

1. The extent to which an author is merely describing a therapeutic technique, or is putting forward a model of group dynamics valid for any kind of group;

2. his underlying orientation in personality theory;

3. his conception of the 'fit' between individual personality and group dynamics;

4. his conception of the roles of patient, and therapist;

5. the degree to which his interpretations rely exclusively upon the 'here and now' situation.

Slavson

Slavson has described (1943, 1947) work in which the group is used as a treatment tool, but the individual is the treatment focus. His theoretical framework is constructed on Freudian ego-psychology as developed in one-to-one psychotherapy, and the dynamics at work in the group situation are regarded as identical: transference formation, catharsis, insight and/or ego strengthening, and reality testing. The therapist treats the individual in the group by support, clarification, and interpretation. He attends to one patient at a time, and although he may try to make his interventions significant for other patients as well, it is always the individual, not the

78

group as such, which remains the centre of his attention.

The group situation is seen as having certain advantages over a one-to-one situation. Treatment is speeded up as the group members have a 'catalytic' effect on one another. Members feel themselves to be in competition with each other for the therapist's love and attention, and sibling rivalry encourages each to do all he can to please the therapist, thus enhancing the positive transference. Change is hastened by the desire to be accepted by the group as well as by the therapist. The members accept interpretations and guidance from each other more readily than they do from the therapist, and initially certain members relate more easily to their peers than to him. At the same time, the support of the other members of the group enables the patient to feel less overawed by the therapist than in a one-to-one situation. This helps the expression of feelings hostile to the therapist which may be partly dispersed on other group members. The discharge of this hostility is therapeutic, decreasing the patient's resistance. By sharing their problems with each other the members discover that they are not unique, which is especially valuable when they suffer from neurotic guilt. Lastly, the group provides each member with a tangible social reality in a 'controlled' setting, and participation modifies attitudes and behaviour. The group experience can improve the patient's social competence, and enable him to learn 'the fundamentals of social living'.

The therapist is 'neutral' but not 'passive'. He responds to the needs of individual members, questioning, discussing directly and indirectly and interpreting. The therapist should adopt an attitude of unconditional love towards the group members, but Slavson distinguishes between acceptance, toleration, and sanction, saying that he accepts every thing, tolerates much, but sanctions little. One way of dealing with hostile acts is by withholding recognition from them by not noticing them, whereas a prohibition would generate more aggression. The group usually exercises its own control, but in the more structured settings the therapist makes clear to the group that certain rules apply. As the group members come to feel secure in their relationship to the therapist they develop a greater toleration of frustration.

The therapist should avoid humour as this arouses the members' aggression. He must also avoid favouring certain members, since this attracts the jealousy and hostility of the others. He should resist the temptation to intervene to protect a member from attack, which might confirm this member's impression of his own inadequacy and deprive him of a learning situation. On the other hand, the therapist should be aware that hostility to a group member is often disguised hostility to himself.

While it is usually therapeutic to motivate the discharge of hostility, the therapist should beware of provoking the 'group hysteria' response, a mob reaction, or unreasoned instinctive regressive response of an intense nature. If it occurs there is a danger that the group may get out of hand and render therapy impossible, and the therapist should close the session. Group hysteria may be the outcome of faulty selection, with the result that the therapist cannot restore 'group equilibrium' after a hostile outburst. Selection should take into account the setting and the personality of the therapist, and both similarity and differences in symptoms are useful.

The group's purpose is to effect a transition from an infantile to a group super-ego. The parentally-derived super-ego, based on fear, is modified by the development of a socially-derived group super-ego, based on positive identifications, 'willing accommodation' and the desire for acceptance. The attitude of acceptance by the therapist reduces the anxiety arising both from destructive impulses and from the fear of punishment and rejection. An attitude of approval is better than words, as approval openly expressed is often too hard for a child with a history of rejection to bear. The absence of condemnation of aggressive behaviour and the opportunities for creative self-expression through participation in the group counteracts self-blame and deflated self-evaluation. As self-acceptance develops, so does acceptance of others and acceptance by the group.

Foulkes

The 'group-analytic' theory of Foulkes and his collaborators, though based on the work of Freud, has been influenced by the theories of Lewin and gestalt psychology. The therapist's attention is focused primarily upon the interpersonal or 'transpersonal' relationships between the members of the group and not exclusively upon the internal psychodynamics of individual patients. All kinds of communications between members of the group, and the responses to these, are considered relevant, and as having their meaning within the total communication network of the group, which is called the 'matrix'. The following account is derived from Foulkes and Anthony (1957).

In the group situation, the therapist cannot analyse the transference of the individual patient in such detail, nor reveal so much of the origins of his disturbance, as in one-to-one therapy. If analysis in depth is what the patient needs then he should not be placed in a group. On the other hand, the group situation is closer to the patient's real life situation, gives a much better insight into his modes of action and reaction, and has a more direct effect upon the patient's current behaviour than does one-to-one therapy. The presence of several persons makes it easier to see the effect of other people upon the individual patient, and the patient's transferences will be more clearly manifested; transferences on to other members sometimes recreate the patient's family situation in a dramatically evident way. Yet while the transference relationship is important, in the group situation one can also work with reality relationships, the 'here and now' situation. The group is a corrective experience, 'ego-training in action'.

Foulkes regards neurosis as evidence of a block in communication, and the production of symptoms as an ambivalent desire to communicate the problem to other people. The task of the therapist and of the group is to 'translate' these symptoms into the real underlying problems, by making conscious the unconscious content of the communications within the group. The process is thus parallel to that in one-to-one psychotherapy, but with the difference that all the group members participate actively in the therapy.

The therapist brings this about by creating a special psychological environment in the group. He makes explicit the purpose of the group and achieves a reduction in the 'censorship' of unconscious thoughts normal in social groups by encouraging the frank disclosure of personal feelings and experience, which the patients soon recognise to be beneficial. The therapist does not guide the discussion but encourages the patients to say whatever comes to mind. Every communication is considered relevant and the therapist's interpretations bring everything back to the group situation in terms of the 'here and now'.

82

After a short time the group members begin to think in a psychological way, applying this procedure themselves. After a few meetings they begin to make interpretations directly to each other, and the therapist then intervenes less, adopting the role of 'participant observer', reserving his own interpretations for the moments when the members come together for the implicit purpose of attacking, defeating, seducing, and escaping from, him. The therapist consistently interprets the group response to himself and encourages the members to participate by turning questions, addressed to himself, back to the group. He also gives all interpretations to the group and not to individual members. He accepts the various transferences which the members put upon him, but resists the group's immature need for an authoritarian leader, indicating what is required by his attitude rather than by instructions.

This technique of 'minimal interference' encourages the development from a 'leader-centred' to a 'group-centred' group. There is a decline in the egocentricity of the patients, who gain a new ability to communicate directly with each other instead of through the therapist alone. The result is mutual support and the sharing of problems. The mental activity required for communicating and understanding others' communications is very therapeutic. 'Active' therapists, on the other hand, produce authoritarian groups where the patterns of communication show little change.

Apart from declining to take an authoritarian role, the therapist must also resist the patients' efforts to make him become a 'sick therapist', a patient like themselves. Although there is frequent pressure on him to do so, there is a co-existent fear that this might happen, making the group leaderless.

As regards the selection of patients for groups the therapeutic potential of the group is believed to be at its highest when the range of diagnoses and disturbances among the members is as wide as the cohesion of the group will stand. The most practicable way of arranging the membership is to introduce new members at long intervals to replace losses.

The 'free-floating discussion' in the group parallels the 'free association' of one-to-one psychotherapy. Communications tend to be in the form of associations, interpretations or defensive reactions. Resistance to therapy comes from the patient himself, who wants his suffering removed without co-operating in any basic changes. It also comes from the influence of the other people involved in his life.

Conflict is pervasive in the group situation, and Foulkes regards one of its most prominent sources as the conflict over 'dominance' in each individual, beginning with parent-child dominance. This may be manifested in the group by conflicts over, for instance, conformity, authority, dependency and change. A patient may be driven, by factors in his personality, into excessive conformity to the group norms, or alternatively into exaggerated individuality. Ambivalent attitudes to authority are seen in the 'father transference' towards the therapist, and good feelings are always counterbalanced by hostility, which is seldom openly expressed because of castration fears. Conflicts over dependency are especially prominent in the early stages when the group goes through a phase of bewilderment and resentment because the therapist declines to take an authoritarian role. The conflict over change is based on the fear that change will eliminate the patient's individuality. Small inner changes, giving rise to continuing therapeutic changes even after the group has ended, are more important than dramatic external changes.

A number of phenomena are distinguished in the group situation which do not necessarily occur in one-to-one therapy. 'Socialisation' of the patient occurs as he participates in the accepting therapeutic group and gradually learns to communicate and receive communications on a meaningful level, counteracting his sense of isolation and inadequacy. The 'mirror' phenomenon is the reflection of himself which the patient finds in the reactions to his presence and actions of the other members of the group. This phenomenon, which enables him to achieve a self-image and a truer sense of identity, is one of the most important therapeutic agents in the group. The 'condenser' phenomenon is the sudden discharge of previously unconscious material which follows the pooling of associated ideas in the group. There is an element of surprise because of the absence of conscious causal connections. The 'chain' phenomenon occurs at the tense moments in the group when 'condenser' themes are released and the 'free-floating discussion' takes the form of each member in turn adding an individual association to the common theme. This can deepen the level of communication in the group and lead to dynamic developments; it is best for the therapist not to join in since he may inadvertently bring the chain to a premature halt. 'Resonance' is the way in which each individual patient will respond to a group event according to his own individual level of fixation.

The opening stages of all groups are characterised by 'theorising'. The theories adopted by the patients to explain their difficulties usually substitute precipitating causes for the predisposing ones, and symptoms tend to be seen as having a single, concrete and external cause. The therapist must resist the temptation to teach didactically, and allow the patients to begin with their theories and to discover their own improvements. 'Support' in the group implies giving the individual the courage to relax his repressions and express hitherto forbidden thoughts, reconditioning the super-ego structure, and helping him to face the cause of his neurotic conflicts. The group soon 'diagnoses' the role habitually played by a member (e.g. the favourite, the attention-seeker,) and its interpretations bring about favourable changes. 'Sub-grouping' which may lead to contacts outside the group meeting is a phenomenon of most groups and usually resolves itself with time. The therapist does not intervene unless it establishes itself so strongly as to be an obstacle to the group's progress. 'Silence' has many different meanings and represents a valuable communication. The therapist should accept it and endeavour to understand its meaning.

The 'scapegoat' may meet a need in the group to transfer away from the therapist feelings they have about him which they are afraid to express directly. This role may also meet a need, in the chosen individual, to be punished. The 'stranger' response is made to the new member in the group who threatens the established familiarity by his disturbing strangeness, and the group attempts to either assimilate or extrude him. The group needs time to assimilate a member and the situation is analogous to the arrival of a new sibling in a family. The therapist should resist the temptation to show the new member undue attention as this will provoke the other members' hostility. The 'historian' is a member who leads the group in reminiscences about the group's past, which may last for several sessions. This is a regressive and defensive phenomenon which may be provoked by the arrival of a 'stranger'. Groups alternate between periods of progress and periods of integration.

The group may develop certain patterns of interaction stemming from the drives and defences of individual members. In addition, 'complementary transactions' take place, interactions between members reflecting reactions within the individual which are of a double nature. The group situation enables these opposite elements to be expressed by different individuals. Among the most common are those between voyeurism and exhibitionism: between hetero- and homosexuality, each interest appearing to predominate in turn: between sadism and masochism: those involved in male-female competitiveness: between manic and depressive feelings: and between progressive and regressive forces in the group. There is often a wish to reverse roles. Certain feelings are transferred on to the therapist.

Bion

In the following two sections, technical terms cannot all be explained or defined. Students are referred to the forthcoming work on Melanie Klein, in this series.

'Basic assumption' theory focuses the attention of the therapist on the group as an entity, as though he is carrying out treatment of the group: it is linked to the object-relations theories of Klein and Fairbairn.

Bion believes that any group of individuals which has met together for the purpose of work, shows mental functioning designed to further the work in hand, which he calls 'work-group activity'. In addition, this 'rational' activity is sometimes hindered, and occasionally furthered, by emotional drives of obscure origin. At these times, the members of the group seem to behave as though they hold an unconscious 'basic assumption' about its aims.

87

There are three possible basic assumptions, fighting or flight, pairing and dependency. If one of these basic assumptions is active at a given moment, the other two will be latent, and the group tends to move from one to another. Bion's theory is applicable to all human groups, and to every individual in all situations, since the individual exists as a member of groups from the beginning of his life, so that even if a group is not present in reality, it is present in the individual's inner phantasy. The advantage in group treatment is that the mechanisms at work are more clearly demonstrable.

The basic assumptions derive from, and attempt to explain, three emotional states into which the group may fall, associated with splitting and projective indentifications. 1, States of rage, aggressiveness, hostility, or fear, from which is derived the basic assumption, 'People come together as a group for the purposes of preserving the group'. This form of organisation seems to know only two techniques of self-preservation, fight or flight. 2, States of optimism and hopeful anticipation, which give rise to the pairing group organisation. When two people become involved in discussion, there is an assumption, on their part and on the group's part, that 'They have come together for sexual purposes'. 3, States of dependency and awe, from which the assumption is derived that 'There is one person in a position to supply the needs of the group, and that the remainder are in a position where their needs are supplied'.

Participation in basic assumption activity is instantaneous, inevitable and instinctive, requiring no training, experience, or mental development. Bion describes the individual's capacity for involuntary combination with other individuals, for sharing and acting on a basic assumption, as a 'valency'. It is a function of the 'basic assumption'
88

form of organisation that when under its influence the group to some extent withdraws from contact with reality. It loses any conception of time, becomes adverse to learning by experience and adapting to the environment, and its language becomes a mode of action rather than of thought, which entails the loss of ability to symbolise or conceptualise.

Both leader and led are forced to play roles involving a relative loss of individual personality and neglect of individual needs. A leader tends to arise in the same instantaneous and involuntary way as the basic assumption grouping itself. He may be a member, an outsider, an individual as yet unborn, or even an idea, a book of laws, or a record of past experiences.

Basic assumption groupings offer security but cannot permanently satisfy individual members. They will attempt to deal with the tensions arising from this fact by trying to locate the source of the unpleasant feelings in other persons or things, rather than admit that they are a function of the group membership which gives security. The change from one kind of basic assumption grouping to another is accompanied by a short period of relief before the tensions break out again.

The fight/flight grouping requires a leader with paranoid tendencies who can point out the enemy and mobilise the members for defence. In the therapeutic group, the enemy is neurosis, and therefore mention of individual psychological problems threatens the group and the offending person is ostracised or attacked. The members may also come together as a fight/flight group because of hostility aroused by the therapist's interpretations, and part of the leader's function is then to express the group's anger and jealousy of the therapist. While fight/flight organisation

89

offers security, the neglect of individual needs renders it
unstable.

The pairing organisation may grow out of the fight/flight
grouping as this assumption also means that the group
must reproduce in order to survive as a group. The pairing
group is suffused with optimism towards the future, and
the leader is the unborn individual or idea, the offspring of
the pair. The two members involved in discussion together
may be either of the same sex or of the opposite sex. But
the delegation of discussion to two individuals inhibits the
others and entails instability in the group.

In the dependency grouping the therapist is treated as an
omniscient parental figure from whom magical solutions
emanate. At the same time, the group shows that it thinks
that he does not know his job, and he is therefore under a
double pressure to adopt an authoritarian role. Feelings are
fairly freely expressed, as there is an assumption that the
parent-figure will not allow them to get out of hand, but
members really communicate only with the therapist and
not with each other. The therapist must resist the temptation to give individual therapy when they bring out prepared statements which they feel are appropriate communications between doctor and patient. Trying to maintain the illusion that they are being cared for by an omniscient magician, they attempt to ignore anything the therapist says which does not fit in with this belief. They are
hostile to work activity and may react with silences, which
deny the therapist the material he needs, or may be expres-
sions of worshipful devotion and awe. Or the group may
deal with the therapist by treating him as dependent, and
choosing the sickest member present as a substitute leader,
addressing all communications to him, and encouraging
him by saying that he keeps the group going and is an

improvement on the therapist. Instability in the dependency grouping stems from resentments inherent in the parent-child relationship, the need for dependency and the desire for independence. There is guilt about greed for parental care, and the attribution of omniscience to one person involves feelings of inadequacy and frustration in the others. Their relief at being able to express their feelings more easily, if only to the therapist, conflicts with their desire to be more mature.

Basic assumption groupings are a necessary part of group life and source of mental energy in the group, but conflicting with them is the patient's conscious desire for the 'work' group structure, reality-orientated around a specific task. One of its aims is a more realistic perception of its environment, and it expresses the need to learn, develop and mature by responding to the group experience and conceptualising from it.

The therapist tries to maintain the work group structure. He must understand the forces motivating the group interactions in order to play off against each other the emotions and needs responsible for the emergence of basic assumption groupings. He interprets only that part of the individual's communications which is relevant to the basic assumption groups forming, making basic assumption activity conscious to the members. He demonstrates the way in which the tensions arising from basic assumption activity are denied, split off or projected onto other individuals or outsiders. When the attempt to keep the group rational fails, he is rejected, as the type of leadership he provides is irrelevant and his refusal to collude with demands for leadership of the basic assumption type is an additional cause of the instability of these formations. Interpretations may work during the sessions but are frequently ignored and do their work between sessions. By making basic assumption activity explicit the therapist enables the patients to feel less threatened by, and more aware of, the forces for development or regression within themselves.

Ezriel

Ezriel has developed an original approach to group therapy based on Bion's theory and Ferenczi's work on the analysis of the transference.

He believes that when people meet in a group, each person tries to project his unconscious phantasy objects upon other members and to manipulate them accordingly. But a member will only stay in a role assigned to him by another if it happens to coincide with his own unconscious phantasy and if it allows him to manipulate others into appropriate roles. Otherwise he will try to twist the discussion until the real group does correspond to his phantasy group. In trying to do this the members will soon establish a 'common group tension' which represents the common denominator of the dominant unconscious phantasy in each member's mind, and which therefore becomes the unconsciously determined topic of conversation in the group. In the interaction which is concerned with resolving this tension, each member takes up a role which is characteristic for his personality structure, in that it corresponds to his specific way of defending himself against the unconscious fears aroused by the common group problem.

The therapist's passive and non-directive attitude enables the common group tension to establish itself in both its unconscious and its manifest though disguised forms. He interprets it to the group in 'here and now' terms and then interprets to each member that aspect of his behaviour in the group which is concerned with the common group tension. The part of the individual's behaviour which is due to individual problems and is not relevant to the common group tension is not interpreted, and attempts by patients to get the therapist to give 'private' interviews in the group by bringing out 'tempting' material may be interpreted as attempts to seduce the therapist into a relationship which excludes the rest of the group. The therapist can control the group by interpretations, avoiding the necessity for making rules for its behaviour. He must interpret the sexual elements in communication or the patients may become too tense and guilty to continue.

The therapist should always ask himself 'What makes the patient behave towards me in this particular way at this moment?' It is unnecessary for the therapist's interpretations to make explicit the link between 'here and now' behaviour and the patients' past experiences as patients will do this linking themselves. The therapist gives his interpretation when he can distinguish three kinds of relationship in the patients' communications. These are, first, the one which the patient tries to establish with the therapist. Ezriel calls this the 'required' relationship, since the patient requires it in order to avoid the second, which is accordingly called the 'avoided' relationship. This he feels he has to avoid in external reality because he is convinced that if he gave in to his secret desire of entering into it this would inevitably lead to the third relationship, a 'calamity'. For example, patients may idealise the therapist in order to avoid expression of angry feelings towards him as they are convinced that this would lead to his rejecting them from the group.

When the 'avoided' relationship is made explicit by interpretation to the group, the individual patient must be told why he is acting in this way in preference to other ways of dealing with the common group problem. This induces a process of 'reality testing' and the patient can be helped to assess the true effects of the avoided relationship by comparing them with the unconsciously expected calamity, which has not materialised. The patient becomes capable of giving less disguised expression in external reality to his hitherto avoided behaviour pattern, and can make decisions based on the real situation free from the influence of outside fears.

Stock Whitaker and Lieberman

Stock Whitaker and Lieberman are influenced by Bion and by French's 'focal-conflict' theory. They describe neurotic difficulties in terms of a number of 'nuclear conflicts' developed early in the patient's life. The feelings deriving from a nuclear conflict are experienced or expressed in ways relevant to the 'here and now' situation and in this form they are called 'focal conflicts'. Nuclear and focal conflicts comprise three elements: a 'disturbing motive', some wish or impulse deriving from basic aggressive or loving needs; a 'reactive motive', some fear which conflicts with the wish, preventing its gratification or expression; and a 'solution', habitual behaviour which the individual develops in order to cope with the anxiety aroused by repeatedly experiencing these wishes and fears. The individual develops a repertory of habitually used solutions, some of which are maladaptive, and interfere with his reality aims or disrupt his interpersonal relationships.

In a group, the 'here and now' situation gives rise to shared disturbing and reactive motives, a 'group focal conflict'. This is the disguised subject of the discussion, and in order to reduce the anxiety to a tolerable level the members try to establish a unanimously accepted unconscious 'solution'. Successfully established solutions can be either 'restrictive', alleviating fears at the expense of the disturbing wish, or 'enabling', alleviating fears while at the same time allowing some satisfaction of disturbing motives. For example, the therapist's failure to provide the expected directive leadership may encourage the disturbing motive of resentment towards him. This is countered by the reactive motive, fear of his anger, or that he will leave. Eventually the solution of 'angry compliance' may be adopted, alleviating reactive fears while offering some satisfaction of the disturbing motive.

Disturbing motives change more slowly than reactive motives and solutions. In the group a persistent 'theme' usually arises made up of group focal conflicts ocurring around closely related disturbing motives. The course of the discussion will be determined by the individual reactions to these conflicts. Enabling solutions lead to more direct expression of disturbing and reactive motives, while restrictive solutions have the opposite affect. The theme changes either when an enabling solution permits a new disturbing motive to be expressed, or when reactive fears are so aroused that a restrictive solution prohibits satisfaction or expression of the current disturbing motive.

The group's life begins with a brief 'formative phase', a 'first round' of themes, with group conflicts determined by the patient's expectations, the therapist's style, and the composition of the group. A set of restrictive solutions is rapidly established which cope with anxieties about criticism, ridicule, punishment by the therapist, etc. and enables the group to operate in reasonable comfort. The sudden or gradual establishment of this set of solutions or group 'culture' is marked by a sense of relief and of shared commitment to the group.

The 'established phase' follows, the basic themes recurring under expanding cultural conditions as enabling solutions permit more direct expression and franker and wider ranging discussion of feelings. Crucial for this development is the reduction of reactive fears, involving their exploration by the group. There is no reduction in disturbing motives, but the manner of their expression alters as frustration becomes better tolerated and reality factors better appreciated. Enabling solutions gradually predominate, but restrictive solutions never disappear entirely as they are a necessary safety-valve for the group when the level of anxiety rises too high.

Occasionally a personal solution may coincide with a group solution : for example, a patient may dominate the group and this may fit in with other patients' fears of exposing themselves. Usually a habitual personal solution is threatened by a group solution, either because it allows more expression of the disturbing motive than he can tolerate, or because it entails that he experiences the reactive motive in uncomfortably direct and intense form. Then he either tries to dissociate himself by daydreaming or absence, or more constructively, tries to influence the group towards a solution which reduces his anxiety. A group solution is a combination of all individual efforts and therefore unlikely to satisfy anyone completely.

Anxiety is kept within bounds by the group culture of established solutions. This 'margin of safety' provides a therapeutic milieu within which he can test out whether his solutions are as vital to him as he supposes. He is enabled to differentiate between real and fantasied dangers involved in recognising and expressing his impulses. Before he can relinquish a habitual personal solution, he has to experience that the feared consequences do not occur :

96

this emotional experience is crucial, and without it intellectual insight is sterile.

Insight or cognitive understanding, more necessary to some patients than to others, occurs through the provision of new information to the patient. He may obtain this himself through observing others or examining his own role, more usually when enabling solutions operate. Other patients' reactions to him and interpretations of his behaviour may also be helpful, save when they are part of maintaining a restrictive solution. They may then be aimed at bringing a deviant into line, be part of a turn-taking solution in which everyone concentrates on one patient at a time, or be scapegoating. Their aim is then not to help the patient but to maintain the group solution. In these circumstances interpretations are often inaccurate, inappropriate, or sterile, or even (as in the case of scapegoating) take on the quality of accusations, as they are really the interpreter's attack on his own unacceptable feelings. Even if they are true, the destructive spirit in which they are then offered makes the patient defend himself against them.

The therapist has to balance his desire to expand the group culture against the need to keep the patients' anxiety within reasonable limits, as an undue increase in anxiety may result in the establishment of a more restrictive solution than might otherwise have been the case. He must therefore often refrain from interfering with restrictive solutions, particularly in the formative phase. He does interfere with scapegoating solutions which expose one patient to massive anxiety, or with solutions which institute the permanent success of a personal maladaptive solution, insulating a patient from therapeutic experiences.

He should take into account the forces current in the group: if the group focal conflict involves fear that he

97

will retaliate, any interpretation on his part will be perceived as a reprimand, intensifying these reactive fears. At other times the group solution may involve instituting him as an expert, and he will then be listened to with unusual attention.

The therapist, like any member, may prevent the establishment of a solution by withholding his co-operation; this creates more anxiety in the formative than in the established phase. If he interprets a shared disturbing motive before a restrictive solution is established, he may arouse anxiety so that an even more restrictive solution results, and after this his interpretation may be ignored. If he waits until an enabling solution has been established, this kind of interpretation may be useful, but generally after a solution is established it is more effective for the therapist to concentrate on the nature of reactive fears. The therapist may also clarify the nature of a solution, best done when there are signs that it is already arousing anxiety and that some patients are willing to give it up. A comment on a solution can indicate to patients that it is permissible to discuss forbidden topics.

Any interpretations directed at individual patients have their significance for both individual and group. If the therapist interprets the group situation for the benefit of the individual, he should focus on the way in which each individual shares in the group focal conflict, as interpretations are most effective when they refer to current experiences.

Application of psychoanalytic models to social workers' groups

Familiarity with the literature is insufficient preparation for doing psychotherapy, which requires adequate training.

The problems on which it is the task of the social worker's group to work will include a psychotherapeutic component, but will also have an environmental aspect. The worker may sometimes usefully provide clients with information about their environment. He may sometimes take action outside the group, but must be sure that this is reality-based and not the mere acting-out of a group dynamic.

The structure of social work agencies usually ensures that the worker is involved with members outside the group; even if he sees them only in the group situation, he has wider obligations as one of the agency team, as members are often quick to demonstrate. Attempts to encapsulate a group from reality are anti-therapeutic, as any working-through of deeper problems will be done through the worker's role in the here-and-now. The worker should be aware of the interaction between his personality and his role, and should relate as a whole person with both loving and aggressive feelings. As the social worker is more involved with members on a reality level than a psychotherapist is, he must pay more attention to the *content* of a communication, and there are a number of levels on which he may respond.

Feelings towards the worker derive partly from 'transference' from the client's past, but also from fears and positive feelings about his real powers and responsibilities, perceived on the basis of the client's past experience. The client will also have fantasies about these realities, connected in turn to those from his past.

To assist the group towards a clearer perception of reality, the worker will often be involved in clarifying his own role. The member's perception of the agency's function makes certain areas of discussion particularly

99

sensitive. Is the worker there to detect, cure, or punish madness, delinquency, neglect? Just as a psychotherapist is offered anti-therapeutic 'authoritarian' or 'sick' roles, the worker is offered similar roles corresponding to the setting (detective, delinquent; rejecting parent, 'bad' child). Members will perceive interpretations partly as value judgements: and in some problems with which social workers are involved, values or social norms may be more obtrusive than in problems of neurosis. The worker may help the group to develop knowledge about the need for a change in values, and structure the environment so that change is advantageous to the members.

The setting of the social worker's group will partly determine the feelings aroused and the ways in which they are expressed. The worker can be helped to understand the connections between the content and the unconscious elements of communication by Nadel's discussion (1951) of the relationship between psychological and sociological phenomena.

Psychological phenomena have to find a social expression. For instance, feelings in a Probation group may be expressed in terms of the social phenomenon 'crime' by virtue of which the members are recruited. Envy of the worker, expressed indirectly, may take the form of an assertion that the police are all criminals. The worker might begin to understand this type of communication by translating it back into psychological terms.

But social and psychological phenomena also 'interact' with one another, as both have real characteristics. For example, the social phenomenon 'marriage' interacts with certain psychological phenomena of which it is partly a function but which it also influences in terms of associated feelings, repressions, etc. Each setting has particular social phenomena prominently involved with it, and these will partly determine and influence all the kinds of feelings which are aroused in the group.

Homans (1950) analysing the workings of the small group in sociological terms, provides an alternative framework to that of psychoanalysis. This can be a useful way of looking at processes in social workers' groups, particularly in agencies concerned with social control.

Three elements are seen as interacting with each other: the environment, the behaviour of individual members, and the social system of the group.

The social system of the group must help to achieve the central group task, the survival of the group in its environment. This entails both the furtherance of the work task and personal satisfactions for the members. Homans distinguishes 'external' and 'internal' systems. In the 'external system' the norms of behaviour are such as are desired by the management to further the work of the group. Arising out of this, the 'internal system' consists of the personal relationships built up between the members within this framework. The two systems interact with each other.

Individual behaviour is analysed in terms of 'activity' (motor activity), 'interaction' (verbal and non-verbal communication) and 'sentiment' (feelings). Patterns of activity, interaction and sentiment between individuals tend to develop together, save where leadership is part of the behaviour. Leaders initiate interaction for others, and the more frequently this occurs, the more the person of lower rank will feel sentiments of respect or hostility and the interaction be held down to the requirements of the external system. Social rank may be based on constituted authority, but may also accrue from close conformity to the norms of the group.

Resentment of those in authority may cause those of lower rank to differentiate themselves away from the norms which these represent. This process is held in check by the interest all members have in conforming to some extent to the norms of the external system, or, ultimately, by sanctions in the environment. Some control is inherent in the norm of 'reciprocity'—if you do not do what the leader wants, he may fail to do you a favour when you need it.

But pressure to conform to group norms is very strong, as activity, interaction and sentiment react upon each other to produce a cumulative negative effect upon the deviant. Hence control is inherent in the system itself and does not involve any special activity. Deviation may entail loss of social rank insofar as this corresponds to conformity to norms. particularly where it brings down negative sentiment or interaction from the leaders, who have the largest influence on social rank. Thus control can also be seen in terms of 'distribution' of rewards by the leaders. The balance between deviation and conformity to the norms promoted by the leaders is adjusted by each individual to obtain maximum satisfaction of his sentiments. 'Authority' (control over others) only exists insofar as it is effective, hence the leader will only give instructions which will be to some degree obeyed. In promoting change, the leader must choose the path involving least conflict.

8
Suggested reading

General theory

Freud (1955) made an important preliminary study employing his usual antithesis between the individual and society, commenting on earlier work by Le Bon (1922) and McDougall (1921). Jung considered group therapy to have only limited value: his position is stated in a published letter to Illing (1963). Burrow, a disciple who made intensive studies of group experience, anticipated and influenced much subsequent development. His work might conveniently be approached via the exegis by Syz (1963).

Through Lewin (1935) (1948) (1952) the perspective of gestalt psychology has played a major part in small group research. A useful critique is found in Nadel (1951). Research produced by the 'Group Dynamics' school includes the well known study of the influence of different styles of leadership on group behaviour by Lippitt and White (1952). Cartwright and Zander (1953) provide a general view of the field.

Moreno is another pioneer figure whose original dis-coveries have generated many subsequent developments.

They include the sociometric method of studying relationships in groups (1953) (1956), and the therapeutic techniques of psychodrama and sociodrama in which patients become aware of new capacities in themselves by acting in unfamiliar roles (1948 and 1959). He has found that groups possess two alternative structures, the 'sociogroup' for work, and the 'psychegroup' for relaxation.

Bales (1950) has attempted to measure interaction in groups and delineate group roles in terms of his framework of concepts called 'Interaction Process Analysis'. He finds that small groups function best where leadership is shared in a co-operative way between an instrumental leader or 'task specialist' and an expressive leader or 'social-emotional specialist', who maintains group cohesion. A parallel is suggested with the roles of father and mother in the nuclear family. Hare, Borgatta and Bales (1955) describe some of the research developed from Bales' formulations.

Homans (1950) derives his theory from a comparative study of various groups. He includes a simple survey of some philosophical speculations concerning the relation between the individual and society, and a critique of the structural/functional approach. Firth (1951) provides another such critique.

Riecken and Homans (1954) attempt to relate the various approaches to small group research within the rubric of Homan's theory. Another appraisal of the various psychological and sociological schools is the useful survey by Olmsted (1959). Klein (1959) attempts a synthesis.

The description of Slavson's ideas in Chapter 7 is taken from his account (1943) of work in a neighbourhood centre, and in other settings (1947). He later elaborates his theoretical framework (1950) and applies this to work

104

in a variety of agencies (1956). The context of American cultural values should be borne in mind when reading these books. The case illustrations are excellent and the reader will find them illuminating for individual as well as group work, which is congruent with the author's theoretical orientation.

Foulkes (1948) describes group-analytic techniques developing from his wartime experiences. Foulkes and Anthony (1957) provide an account of theory and practice, with case material. An extended description is found in Foulkes (1964).

Bion's theory is advanced in a series of papers now published in book form (1961) showing the progress of his thinking since his wartime work. The theoretical framework of the central papers develops separately from that of the early ones. In the later papers he applies his theory to the analysis of certain institutions within society and to social philosophy. The final papers relate his work to object-relations personality theory.

Ezriel's ideas are described in a number of articles (1950, 1950, 1956, 1959) containing case material, some of which reflect his wider scientific interests.

Stock Whitaker and Lieberman (1964) provide a comprehensive statement of the focal-conflict approach developed from French (1952). They delineate the differing preoccupations of therapist and social psychologist, and compare various theories of group therapy.

For workers with clients involved in unfavourable subcultures, Cartwright (1951) demonstrates how resistant the individual is to changing in any way contrary to group pressures. He advocates making groups the targets of and agents for change, by opening up communications and making information about the need for, plans for, and consequences of, change, the accepted property of the group. Cressey (1955) combines this concept of behaviour as the property of groups with Sutherland's theory of differential association (1947) to develop a sociological, non-psychiatric theory of changing behaviour through membership of groups with favourable values. Volkman (1965) analyses a self-help organisation (Synanon) in terms of Cressey's concepts. Scarpitti and Stephenson (1966) describe their application to groups of delinquents.

Group work in institutions

Maxwell Jones (1952) and Rapoport (1960) have described attempts to create therapeutic communities in mental hospitals. Miller (1964) describes psychosocial treatment of a group of boys in a residential hostel. Fenton (1957, 1967) has had considerable influence on group counselling techniques in penal institutions, though Morrison (1961) argues that Fenton exaggerates the permissive aspects of his approach. De Berker (1956) indicates some of the issues facing staff with authoritarian traditions, and (1963) describes the effect on an institution of opening up communications through group counselling. Bishop (1960) shows how group counselling in a Borstal led to shared responsibility for improved behaviour. Tollinton (1966) describes measures to reduce staff-inmate subcultures in a psychiatric prison.

Howard Jones (1960) describes the operation of a school for maladjusted boys using group therapy and an organisational structure designed to produce a pro-reform sub-culture. He reviews theories of group dynamics and analyses earlier institutional experiments in several countries. There is a discussion of group work with case material.

Family group therapy

Bell (1963) advances a theoretical framework in which the family is viewed, in its social and cultural context, as a network of interaction and communication. The tasks of the family demand flexibility and the aims of individuals must support the group as a group. The 'sick' family exhibits rigidity and impoverishment of communications and the therapist demonstrates new ways of participating and communicating, disrupting unsatisfactory patterns and eliminating role ambiguity.

Bowlby (1949) describes an adaptation of Bion's theory to interviewing all members of the family together. The emphasis is again on communication, as the overt family row which develops in the clinic occurs in a more fragmented and inferential form at home. The therapeutic forces are sustained by the desire of all members of the family to live more comfortably together.

Skynner (1967) uses the concept of the 'minimum sufficient network' of communications between individuals to be included in the treatment process. He describes families who distribute ego-functions between members and social agencies, so that therapy involves improving communication between them.

Parsloe (1967) describes the long-term treatment of a multi-problem family by regular home visits, in which the worker at first 'acted out' her concern in tangible ways, the confidence generated leading to the inclusion of more and more members of the family in the interviews, with improving verbal communication.

Learning in groups

Ottaway (1966) describes a method of 'teaching' psychology by slowly 'feeding' theory to students in a T-group situation, stimulating emotional learning superior to intellectual understanding alone.

Balint (1957), teaching psychotherapy to groups of general practitioners, focuses on the counter-transference. In contrast, Irvine (1959) teaches casework to groups of social workers by focusing on the understanding of the client as presented by the worker. She indicates the relationships between leader, group, client and member presenting the case, and differences between teaching and therapy. Gosling and Turquet (1967) treat these topics in detail and indicate ways in which the leader can utilise 'basic assumption' energy to further the group task. In the same volume, Woodhouse describes a course on marital interaction for groups of social workers, and Miller the use of small groups in training Borstal staff. The same author (1966) details a training scheme for Approved School staff within the institutional setting. Howard Jones (1966) depicts training for prison officers which is related to their role in their organisation and in the wider society.

Trist and Sofer (1959) describe a course designed to improve the understanding of interpersonal and inter-group relationships, including a detailed account of the 'Study Group' method, which consists of the group examing its own behaviour in the 'here and now', with the aid of a consultant. Bradford, Gibb and Benne (1964) describe the more didactic T-group methods developed in the U.S.A. Higgin and Bridger (1965) analyse and exercise in inter-group relations in terms of a division of function between groups in their shared emotional and work task. Rice (1965) describes various courses, providing a theoretical framework.

Crichton (1962) summarises much material relevant to

both group relations training and to the organisation of work groups.

Organisations and work groups

Study groups and inter-group experiences are aids to the understanding of organisations as systems of inter-group and inter-personal relations. Rice (1963) offers a framework of principles of organisation based on analysis of operations involved in its primary task. A good general handbook on organisation is March (1958). Of general interest are Schein (1965) Crozier (1964), Etzioni (1964) a brief general introduction, and Blau and Scott (1965) whose illustrative material is drawn from social work organisations. Social workers have concentrated their attention on their relationship to their clients to the neglect of studying how these are affected by their own organisational structure : there is a need for a more all-round view. Menzies (1967) describes how hospital nursing organisation acts as a defence against anxiety, to the detriment of job satisfaction and patient care. Homans (1950) contains material on the internal structure of work groups derived from the Hawthorne Experiments. Extended consideration of the optimal principles of work group organisation is found in Trist, *et al* (1963), a study of a reorganisation in coal mining in which each group has autonomy, its own leadership and responsibility for its own task, with maximum interchangeability of roles. Management is then in an advisory rather than a controlling role.

A parallel area of neglect is the effect of the structure of the client's work group on his other relationships. Dennis *et al* (1956) vividly describe the correspondence between work and family relationships in a coal-mining community.

Sofer (1961) describes work as a 'social consultant' to various organisations, making use of small group discussions to clarify problems and roles. Psychotherapy concentrates on 'inner change', but social consultancy involves an active advisory component, presenting clients with new facts about the environment. He describes the inter-group relations involved in change.

Social Groupwork

The following seem likely to be of most help to the student.

Davies (1966) describes a discussion group of deprived adolescent boys in care in a hostel. The leader introduced a topic but did not otherwise guide the discussion. In spite of these boys' severe difficulties, they developed a clearer grasp of reality, improved ability to relate to others, and to communicate with authority figures. Roberts (1962) describes discussion groups for long-stay foster-parents which helped to clarify the roles of child care officer, foster parent and natural parent. Sharing feelings about being foster-parents led to some useful working-through, and was evidently therapeutic for some members. Rowe (1966) advocates a limited use of groups in the selection of adopters.

Brueton (1963) describes an unstructured discussion group for adolescent girls attending a skin clinic. Sharing feelings broke down the members' isolation and there was an improvement in both their physical symptoms and their interpersonal relationships.

Barr (1966) surveys the present practice of groupwork by probation officers, producing much valuable material. Fears that, by meeting in groups, clients may be led to commit offences together, are assuaged by the finding that this happened only once in 72 different groups. Ashley

(1962) traces the development of a group of adolescent boys on probation and answers objections as to 'contamination', 'loss of authority' and 'getting too deep'. A later article (1965) describes a group of adolescents of both sexes on probation, relating development to Bion's theory and to Slavson's ideas on group leadership. Freegard (1964) gives an account of a group of adolescent girls on probation, commenting on the leader's role, and the working-through of problems of authority and identity. McCullough (1963) describes a group of adolescent girls in a probation hostel, examining the leader's role, the development of the group, mutual support, and the vicarious working-through which occurs as members hear of others' experiences and observe their behaviour in the group.

Munro (1952) describes a group of parents at a Child Guidance Clinic. Sheppard, (1960) describing hospitalised schizophrenics whose ability to communicate improved through group experience, emphasises their need for protection, support and permanence. Wildman (1967) describes family group interviews as a method of treating withdrawn adolescents, the therapist taking an active role, pointing out denial, etc., to improve communications.

Problems of space prohibit an adequate treatment of the material produced by youth workers. Smith (1966) analyses the techniques and problems of 'problem-centred' youth work. Biven and Holden (1966) give a good description of the interaction of intergroup and inter-personal relations in an unattached cafe project. Heap (1966) gives examples of ways in which the leader can deal with scapegoating by influencing the group towards accepting their projected feelings.

McKenzie (1961) has produced a useful guide for running marriage preparation discussion groups.

Bibliography

ASHLEY, P.D. (1962) 'Group Work in the Probation Setting', *Probation*, Vol. 10, No. 1, March.

ASHLEY, P. D. (1965) 'The Development of a Mixed Group', *Probation*, Vol. 11, No. 3, November.

BALES, R. F. (1950) *Interaction Process Analysis*, Cambridge, Massachusetts: Addison-Wesley.

BALES, R. F., HARE, A. P. and BORGATTA, E. (1955) *Small Groups. Studies in Social Interaction*, New York: Knopf.

BALINT, M. (1957) *The Doctor, his Patient and the Illness*, London: Pitman Medical.

BARR, H. (1966) *A Survey of Group Work in the Probation Service*, H.M.S.O.

BELL, J. E. (1963) 'Recent Advances in Family Group Therapy', in Rosenbaum, M. and Berger, M., eds., *Group Psychotherapy and Group Function*, New York: Basic Books.

BION, W. R. (1961) *Experiences in Groups*, London: Tavistock.

BISHOP, N. (1960) *Group Work at Pollington Borstal*, Howard League.

BIVEN, B. and HOLDEN, H. M. (1966) 'Informal Youth Work in a Cafe Setting', *Howard Journal*, Vol. XII, No. 1.

BLAU, P. M. and SCOTT, R. W. (1963) *Formal Organisations*, Routledge & Kegan Paul.

BOWLBY, J. (1949) 'The Study and Reduction of Group Tensions in the Family', *Human Relations*, Vol. II, 123-128.

BRADFORD, L. P., GIBB, J. R. and BENNE, K. D. (1964) *T-Group Theory and Laboratory Method*, New York: Wiley.

BRUETON, M. (1963) 'An Experiment in Group Work with Adolescent Skin Patients', *The Almoner*, Vol. 15, No. 12, March.

BURROW, T. See SYZ, H.

CARTWRIGHT, D. (1951) 'Achieving Change in People. Some Applications of Group Dynamics Theory', *Human Relations*, Vol. 4, 381-392.

CARTWRIGHT, D. and ZANDER, A. (1953) eds., *Group Dynamics, Research and Theory*, Tavistock.

CRESSEY, D. R. (1955) 'Changing Criminals: The Application of the Theory of Differential Association', *American Journal of Sociology*, Vol. LXI, 116-120.

CRICHTON, A. (1962) *Personnel Management and Working Groups*, Institute of Personnel Management.

CROZIER, M. (1964) *The Bureaucratic Phenomenon*, London: Tavistock.

DAVIES, J. W. D. (1966) 'Group Work and the Deprived Child', *Case Conference* Vol. 12, No. 7, January.

DE BERKER, P. (1956) 'Staff Strain in Institutions', *British Journal of Delinquency*, Vol. VI, No. 4, April.

DE BERKER, P. (1963) 'Group Counselling in Penal Institutions', *British Journal of Criminology*, Vol. IV, No. 1, July.

DENNIS, N., HENRIQUES, F. and SLAUGHTER, R. C. (1956) *Coal is our life*, London: Eyre and Spottiswoode.

ETZIONI, A. (1964) *Modern Organisations*, New Jersey: Prentice-Hall.

EZRIEL, H. (1950) 'A Psychoanalytic Approach to Group

Treatment', *British Journal of Medical Psychology*, Vol. XXIII, 51-74.

EZRIEL, H. (1950) 'A Psychoanalytic Approach to the Treatment of Patients in Groups', *Journal of Mental Science*, Vol. XCVI, 774-779.

EZRIEL, H. (1956) 'Experimentation Within the Psychoanalytic Session', *British Journal for the Philosophy of Science*, Vol. VII, 29-48.

EZRIEL, H. (1959) 'The Role of Transference in Psychoanalytic and Other Approaches to Group Treatment', *Acta Psychotherapeutica*, Vol. VII, 101-116.

FENTON, N. (1957) *What Will be Your Life?* New York: American Correctional Association.

FENTON, N. (1967) *The Correctional Community*, University of California Press.

FIRTH, R. (1951) *Elements of Social Organisation*, London: Watts & Co.

FOULKES, S. H. (1948) *Group-Analytic Psychotherapy*, London: Heinemann.

FOULKES, S. H. and ANTHONY, E. J. (1957) *Group Psychotherapy*, London: Penguin.

FOULKES, S. H. (1964) *Therapeutic Group Analysis*, London: Allen and Unwin.

FREEGARD, M. (1964) 'Five Girls Against Authority', *New Society*, 13th February.

FRENCH, T. M. (1952) *The Integration of Behaviour*, Vols. 1 and 2, Chicago: University of Chicago Press.

FREUD, S. (1955) *Group Psychology and the Analysis of the Ego*, Standard Edition Vol. 18, London: Hogarth Press.

GOSLING, R., MILLER, R. H., TURQUET, P. M. and WOODHOUSE, D. (1967) *The Use of Small Groups in Training*, London: Codicote.

HEAP, K. (1966) 'The Scapegoat Role in Youth Groups', *Case Conference*, Vol. 12, No. 7, January.

HIGGIN, G. and BRIDGER, H. (1965) *Psychodynamics of an Inter-Group Experience*, London : Tavistock.

HOMANS, G. C. (1950) *The Human Group*, New York : Harcourt, Brace & Co.

HOMANS, G. C. and RIECKEN, H. W. (1954) 'Psychological Aspects of Social Structure', in G. Lindsey, ed., *Handbook of Social Psychology*, Vol. II, Cambridge, Massachusetts : Addison-Wesley.

ILLING, H. A. (1963) 'C. Jung on the Present Trends in Group Psychotherapy' in M. Rosenbaum and M. Berger, eds., *Group Psychotherapy and Group Function*, New York : Basic Books.

IRVINE, E. (1959) 'The Use of Small Group Discussion in the Teaching of Human Relations and Mental Health', *British Journal of Psychiatric Social Work*, Vol. V, No. 1.

JONES, HOWARD (1960) *Reluctant Rebels*, London: Tavistock.

JONES, HOWARD (1966) 'Prison Officers as Therapists', *Howard Journal*, Vol. XII, No. 1.

JONES, MAXWELL (1952) *Social Psychiatry: A Study of Therapeutic Communities*, London : Tavistock.

JUNG, C. See ILLING, H. A.

KLEIN, J. (1959) *The Study of Groups*, London : Routledge & Kegan Paul.

LE BON, G. (1922) *The Crowd*, Eng. Trans. London : Fisher Unwin.

LEWIN, K. (1935) *A Dynamic Theory of Personality*, trans. D. K. Adams and K. E. Zener. New York : McGraw-Hill.

LEWIN, K. (1948) *Resolving Social Conflicts*, New York : Harper.

LEWIN, K. (1952) *Field Theory in Social Science*, ed. D. Cartwright, London : Tavistock.

BIBLIOGRAPHY

LIPPITT, R. and WHITE, R. K. (1952) 'An Experimental Study of Leadership and Group Life', in *Readings in Social Psychology*, revised edition, G. Swanson, T. Newcomb and E. Hartley, eds., New York: Henry Holt & Co.

MCCULLOUGH, M. K. (1963) 'Group Work in Probation', *New Society*, 21st February.

MCDOUGALL, W. (1921) *The Group Mind*, London: Cambridge University Press.

MCKENZIE, A. (1961) *Group Discussion with Young People*, London: National Marriage Guidance Council.

MARCH, J. G. (1958) ed. *Organisations*, London: Chapman Hall.

MENZIES, I. E. P. (1967) *The Functioning of Social Systems as a Defence Against Anxiety*, London: Tavistock.

MILLER, D. H. (1966) 'Problems of Staff Training in a School for Delinquent Adolescent Boys', *Howard Journal*, Vol. XII, No. 1.

MILLER, D. H. (1964) *Growth to Freedom*, London: Tavistock; and see GOSLING, R.

MORENO, J. L. (1953) *Who Shall Survive?* New York: Beacon House.

MORENO, J. L. (1956) *Sociometry and the Science of Man*, New York: Beacon House.

MORENO, J. L., *Psychodrama*, New York: Beacon House, Vol. 1 (1948), Vol. 2 (1959).

MORRISON, R. L. (1961) *Group Counselling in Penal Institutions*, London: Howard League.

MUNRO, D. M. G. (1952) 'An Experiment in the Use of Group Methods with Parents In a Child Guidance Clinic', *British Journal of Psychiatric Social Work*, Vol. 12, No. 6.

NADEL, S. F. (1951) *The Foundations of Social Anthropology*, London: Cohen & West.
116

OLMSTED, M. S. (1959) *The Small Group*, New York: Random House.

OTTAWAY, A. K. C. (1966) *Learning Through Group Experience*, Routledge & Kegan Paul.

PARSLOE, P. (1967) 'Working with Families Who Do Not Attend A Clinic', *Papers given at 23rd Annual Child Guidance Inter-Clinic Conference*. National Association for Mental Health.

RAPPOPORT, R. N. (1960) *The Community as Doctor*, London: Tavistock.

RICE, A. K. (1963) *The Enterprise and its Environment*, London: Tavistock.

RICE, A. K. (1965) *Learning for Leadership*, London: Tavistock.

RIECKEN, H. W. See HOMANS, G. C.

ROBERTS, V. (1962) 'An Experiment in Group Work with Foster Parents', *Case Conference*, Vol. 9, No. 6, November.

ROWE, J. (1966) *Parents, Children and Adoption*, London: Routledge & Kegan Paul.

SCARPITTI, F. R. and STEPHENSON, R. M. (1966) 'The Use of the Small Group in the Rehabilitation of Delinquents', *Federal Probation*, Vol. XXX, No. 3, September.

SCHEIN, E. H. (1965) *Organisational Psychology*, New Jersey, Prentice-Hall.

SHEPPARD, M. L. (1960) 'Psychotherapy With a Small Group of Chronic Schizophrenic Patients', *British Journal of Psychiatric Social Work*, Vol. 5, No. 5.

SKYNNER, A. C. R. (1967) 'Diagnosis, Consultation and Co-Ordination of Treatment', in *Papers given at 23rd Annual Child Guidance Inter-Clinic Conference, 1967*, National Association for Mental Health.

SLAVSON, S. R. (1943) *An Introduction to Group Therapy*, New York: Commonwealth Fund.

SLAVSON, S. R. (1947) ed, *The Practice of Group Therapy*, Pushkin Press.

SLAVSON, S. R. (1950) *Analytic Group Psychotherapy*, New York: Columbia Press.

SLAVSON, S. R. (1956) ed, *The Fields of Group Psychotherapy*, New York: International Universities Press.

SMITH, C. S. (1966) 'The Youth Service and Delinquency Prevention', *Howard Journal*, Vol. XII, No. 1.

SOFER, C. (1961) *The Organisation from Within*, London: Tavistock; and see TRIST, E. L.

STOCK WHITAKER, D. and LIEBERMAN, M. A. (1964) *Psychotherapy Through the Group Process*, London: Prentice-Hall.

SUTHERLAND, E. H. (1947) *Principles of Criminology*, New York: Lipincott.

SYZ, H. (1963) 'A Summary Note on the Work of Trigant Burrow', in Rosenbaum, M. and Berger, M., eds., *Group Psychotherapy and Group Function*, New York: Basic Books.

TOLLINTON, H. P. (1966) 'The Psychological Treatment of Abnormal Offenders', *Prison Service Journal*, Vol. V, No. 20, July.

TRIST, E. L., HIGGIN, G. W., MURRAY, H., and POLLOCK, A. B. (1963) *Organisational Choice*, London: Tavistock.

TRIST, E. L. and SOFER, C. (1959) *Exploration in Group Relations*, Leicester University Press.

TURQUET, P. M. See GOSLING, R.

VOLKMAN, R. (1965) 'Differential Association and the Rehabilitation of Drug Addicts', *British Journal of Addiction*, Vol. LXI, November, Pergamon Press.

WILDMAN, M. (1967) 'Communication in Family Therapy', *British Journal of Psychiatric Social Work*, Vol. IX, No. 2.